LESSONS
FROM THE COALFACE

**Learn why Network Marketing continues
to grow, and why a conventional career
may not be your best option.**

ISBN: 978-0-9934762-0-4

First published in 2015

The Coalface

As a young boy growing up in Wales, I was enthralled by the stories of brave young men digging black gold (coal) out of the mountains that surrounded me. Men who worked at the 'Coalface' knew they would only get paid for what they produced. Today just like the terms 'frontline and trenches from the great world wars' the term Coalface is widely and respectfully used to describe someone that understands what its like to feel the pressure of knowing success or failure rests firmly on their shoulders.

Dedication

I want to dedicate this book to all the passionate Network Marketing members that are out there making our industry rock and roll.

You are an amazing group of people, your vision, commitment and passion for your lives never fails to inspire me.

I congratulate you for deciding to be different and live your life the way you choose to live it.

How to read this book.

Make sure you get the most from this book. By all means read it and enjoy it but if you really want to get the most from it get a highlighter pen and mark all the comments that make sense to you.

Grab a pencil and jot down notes on things you need to change or adjust in order to move ahead with your life. Make this book a roadmap to a better future.

CONTENT

CHAPTER 3

My story. It's been a rollercoaster ride. If I can do it, so can you 33

CHAPTER 4

Lessons from the coalface. The qualities you will need to succeed ... 51

CHAPTER 5
Questions, myths and misconceptions about Network Marketing 69

CHAPTER 6
What can you gain from a Network Marketing career? 79

CHAPTER 10
The highs and lows of life as an entrepreneur...................................... **141**

INTRODUCTION

Why did I write this book?

I wrote this book for three reasons.

Firstly, I am passionate about helping others get what they want from life and believe in my ability to help them get it.

Secondly, I want to warn people that getting a job or career and putting all your financial security in the hands of an employer and then believing life will work out great is not the most intelligent plan.

Thirdly, I want to make you aware of a concept called Network Marketing.

Network Marketing has allowed me and millions of other people to develop financial independence and live life the way they choose to live it. Even today it's still one of the best kept secrets in the world.

If you are looking for a new job or change of career I urge you to read every page, I promise it will affect how you think about the rest of your life.

If you have ever dreamt of escaping the rat race and living the life of your dreams by becoming time and money free, you are going to love this book.

There are choices we make early in life that have a massive bearing on where we end up and I for one believe it's important to know all your options. This book is written as a wakeup call, to give you advice on how to survive and thrive in a very competitive world.

There will be no get rich quick nonsense or meaningless text. It will be practical, clear and honest. It's based on the lessons I was forced to learn in order to get ahead in life and the very same lessons I am passing onto my children.

Using the information you are about to read, I have been able to develop a business that continues to supply thousands of happy customers consuming millions of pounds worth of products every year, giving us a lifestyle as a family we could only have dreamt of.

The vast majority of people that actually go on and do anything with the mentoring advice I give them always ask me to say it as it is, without any fluff. So if it's ok with you, I am going to proceed with the assumption that you feel the same way.

Still here? Great, let's go.

In this brief introduction I am going to do all I can to get your attention. I don't want this to be another book you pick up read and take no action. I am not the sort of person who wastes my time or anyone else's and I hope this book will reinforce that many times over.

Life is short at best. As I write this one of my best friends has died from cancer at the age of just forty-two, leaving five kids and a wife behind. Let me be honest with you, that's given me a real sense of urgency and focus to live life to its fullest at every given opportunity and I sincerely hope that reflects in the text that follows.

I am not a trained author or even a skilled writer. I am not going to fill pages with fluffy meaningless text. I am going to say it like it is, warts and all and hope that a little plain talk from someone who's hacked their way through the jungle is just what you need.

I hope you are searching and I mean seriously searching, because if you're not then no matter what I type it's not going to help. You have to have desire and ambition for anything to change. If you can tick those boxes then buckle up. We are going for a ride and I hope this is going to be a page turner that keeps you awake!

As I type I feel genuine excitement for you because I know what's in the pages ahead. At the same time a part of me is a little scared that I may not find the words and phrases that reach out and grab you. Here is what I do know; I am going to give it all I've got. It won't be perfect but it's definitely going to make an impact.

This book is about the highs and lows of life as an entrepreneur and why I turned my back on the conventional job or career route. It's also about the choices ahead of you that will define the life you live. I am also going to tell you my story. The reason for this is because I have made lots of mistakes. If you are bright you will learn from the lessons I share, avoid the mistakes I made, succeed faster than I did, seek me out, buy me a beer and tell me the time I spent on this book was worth it!

Here is the short version of my journey. I started off excited and thought everything would be easy. It wasn't. Everything was much harder than I expected. Lots of ups and downs. Even more twists and turns. The occasional head-on collision (literally), then once I got my head around the rules of the game it was a blast!

If I have one regret. I wish I had learned what's in this book much quicker!

By the time you finish reading, not only will you have a road map through the jungle that's ahead of you, you will also have access to a vehicle that can set you free faster than you could ever have imagined.

CHAPTER 1

CAREERS, JOBS AND WHY NETWORK MARKETING MAY BE YOUR BEST OPTION.

Careers, jobs and why Network Marketing may be your best option.

There is an exciting life in front of you. Whether you are eighteen or eighty I want you to get the absolute best you can from it. The world economy is developing at warp speed and it's not going to slow down.

The pages that follow will highlight the skills you need and the many different pathways available to you. You're going to ask yourself some big questions and the answers you find will dictate the life you lead.

It's also going to stimulate you into questioning exactly what you want from a career and then help you prepare yourself for what lays ahead. Just taking this first step towards learning more is a great move. This book will encourage you to think differently to the rest and help you stand out for all the right reasons.

Changes in the local and global economy have left many people in uncertain positions. There is no easy way to say that morale in many sectors of employment is at an all-time low due to the restructuring of management and resources. Sadly, a fair chunk of the disillusioned people can be found in the frontline services that are the pride of our nation. If you are passionate about entering any of these sectors that are suffering from extensive cutbacks, the truth is they need you but be sure to proceed with your eyes wide open.

Calling all graduates. You have other options. You do not have to follow the nine to five, forty year plan.

If you have recently left university or are about to leave, get ready. It's a battleground out there. With more and more grads entering the marketplace the competition for jobs is hotter than ever. Time and again surveys report that over ninety percent of graduates are not able to get a job in the same field that they did their degree in. In addition to this, national employment statistics reveal up to eighty percent of some graduates are still searching for employment six months after leaving university.

The simple fact is that there are not enough jobs specific to the topics that people are choosing. Unfortunately most graduates only seem to be recognising this when they enter the marketplace. But wait, it's not all doom and gloom and here is the good news. Whole new industries are emerging and you're about to learn what it takes to succeed in them. Prepare yourself and get ready for a change in direction.

"What about me? I am over forty, not sure what to do next and want my life to mean something."

In writing this book I've asked lots of people lots of questions. I've had some amazing conversations with friends and acquaintances that have all asked me to make sure the book reaches out to the over forties. It will and I assure you it's never too late to get started. The feedback has shaped not only what I write but also how I feel about what I write. There is a huge body of people out there who for one reason or another have reached a point in their lives where they are looking for a new challenge.

Hopefully, through the pages that follow, you will realise that your life experience has real value in the market place but only if you decide to use it.

It's not easy to make a new start and I fully understand the emotions involved in trying to break free. I will do all I can to give you the confidence you need. I have helped thousands do this already, so why not you?

One small word of caution though. Life experience tends to come with layers of opinion that get in the way of you gathering all the facts. Your mind is like a parachute. It only works if it's open, so do all you can to keep it that way. Set aside any opinions you may have. If you are looking for permanent change, read on and be open to possibilities.

If you know a businessperson, dare them to read this.

Being self-employed or in business for yourself, whilst very rewarding can also be very tough. Being forced to have a wide range of skills from keeping good books, marketing your business, delivering your service and paying staff can and does present a very big demand on your time and energy. Then the frustration of someone in a job saying to you: "Ah it's ok for you, you're self-employed. You can do what you want." That alone can tip you over the edge after a tough week. If only they knew.

This book is going to appeal to self-employed driven people.

How many business operations do you know that turn over tens of millions with no staff, no overheads, offer huge returns, keep paying you when you don't show up, receive support from a huge parent company brand, no legal headaches, tiny startup costs, no exposure to bad debt, free holidays and amazing parties. Sounds like the description of a perfect business. Surely it's too good to be true.

I dare you to read this book. It's all true. Network Marketing is turning over billions every year and growing like crazy. You just don't know about it yet. While you fight for every inch, someone else has found an astonishing vehicle and it's a businesspersons dream. Soak up every sentence. It may be exactly what you are looking for.

To survive you have to diversify.

I cannot think of a more important title than the one I have just written. People who learn to diversify survive. People who are stuck in their ways and are unable or unwilling to change and develop get tossed aside. Tough but true. As you read on, you are going to find out that developing a Network Marketing business instead of or alongside your chosen career is a simple option to take. It will rapidly develop your skill set and make you stand out and be more attractive than others in the job market.

Why not use a Network Marketing business to pay back your debt quicker, improve your retirement fund or quit your career.

Once you have read the book you will know you have your hands on a business opportunity where you are in control of how much income you decide to make. Unlike a job where your income is fixed, in your new Network Marketing career your income is based on your skill and production and only you set the limits.

As a nation we are drowning in debt and this has to change. As quickly as possible get yourself into a positive cash flow situation and get out of debt. Nobody is going to pay your bills for you. You have to take responsibility and get a plan in place right now. Don't allow yourself to be casual about this. Getting a job and paying off the minimum amounts against your student loans or credit cards will trap you into a lifetime of financial misery. Learn this lesson now and you will never suffer the financial anxiety that plagues the majority of the population.

Be different. Having financial peace of mind is one of the best feelings in the world and worth every bit of effort required to achieve it.

If you are already well into a career path but feel you are at a crossroads, read on and you will find this book will offer you some exciting new routes.

We all become a product of our environment eventually. Grow up in Germany and you will have a German accent. Grow up in France and you will have a

French accent. Hang around negative or sad people and you will become negative and sad. That's just how it is. If you are starting out and are lucky enough to be able to choose your career path, think about those words then try to follow this suggestion.

Look for dynamic, forward-thinking people and organisations that encourage you to learn and develop your skills and grow as a human being.

If you are like most people, you won't have the luxury of being so choosy but at least you now know what you are looking for as you progress and move employers.

Although this book is about entrepreneurship, of course there are also millions of people who do an astonishing job in their chosen professions. So let me pop in a small disclaimer. I have nothing but respect for anyone who is happy with being in a regular nine to five job, year after year. I just knew it wasn't the path for me so I needed to do something about it.

This book is written for people who are looking for a little more freedom of time and expression. People that want to take control of their destiny and find out what's possible for their life. People who for one reason or another don't like the look of the options ahead of them or have ended up in a job they just don't enjoy anymore.

It's extremely rare for people to end up in the precise job they planned for from day one. You're far more likely to end up doing a job that you just seemed to fall into. Years pass by and naturally what you want from life changes. It's easy to feel a little trapped or unhappy. That's just how it is for many people and this book will help you find a route out.

I understand not everyone wants to be an entrepreneur and there is nothing wrong with that. Life would be very boring if we all thought the same. What I can say with confidence is everyone wants to succeed as opposed to fail, so let's look at what successful people do, how they think and then ask yourself which path you want to put yourself on.

Look at the two different life plans below, then choose the one you want.

Here are a few sentences to study carefully and understand how they will apply to your use of time going forward.

Successful people invest time to create assets that generate money.

Unsuccessful people trade time for money (job), spend the money then are forced to trade time for money again (trapped).

If learning and applying that law to your life is all you learn from this book, I promise you it was worth the cover price.

Let's face it, most people work for money, not for the love of the job. Clearly there are exceptions to this, so again I am not trying to offend anyone.

Let's take a look at those two headline sentences once more. I want to make sure you really understand what I have written. When you fully understand these sentences, you will improve how and where you invest your time to create the life that reflects more of what you want.

Let me retype those sentences using more emotive language to try and get them to stick in your mind. They are really important and easy for you to skim over and miss.

Which of the following descriptive sentences matches what you want from life?

LIFE PLAN 1:

People who invest their time into an asset such as a business that generates income even when they are not working means they can leave the rat race behind, travel the world and live the life they choose because they are time and money free.

LIFE PLAN 2:

People who exchange time for money often feel trapped like hamsters in a wheel. Monday morning the alarm clock shakes you out of bed. The chain around your ankle that runs all the way back to your place of work tightens. You're about to get reeled in. The cold wet and windy commute beckons and you count the days to when your boss allows you two weeks of freedom.

It's meant to be a little scary. You're about to make massive decisions that impact your life. You need to concentrate like never before. Please don't be offended by my graphic description. It happens every day. I have met thousands of people who described their life to me in that same fashion saying they wish they had learned these things years ago.

I am writing this as a warning to hopefully save me from having more of those conversations with you.

You have one life and I am going to do my best to help you live it to its absolute fullest potential. It's as simple as that. If I help you avoid the same mistakes I see so many other people make, then my head will hit the pillow very softly tonight.

Myth No. 1: Get a job to create security for you and your family.

Study, work hard, get a good job in a big company or organisation, keep your head down and they will look after you. And the next line is written by Hans Christian Anderson!

Guess what? The sales pitch has been so good, some people still actually believe that line is true. Worse still they actually build their life with this as their foundation and then they are devastated and disappointed in the government or anyone but themselves when their company restructures and their job position is no longer required.

They can't believe it's happened to them. By now they have a young family, a mortgage, a new car on the drive and overnight it all falls apart. Please don't let this happen to you.

The world is reshaping at an astonishing pace and it worries me that so few people understand the real life impact these changes will ultimately have on them. I sincerely hope the above statements do not apply to you and your loved ones but the reality is they are highly likely to.

Here is just a small list of why your job or anyone else's job may be under threat in the future and why it's a good idea to have a backup plan up and running pretty quickly.

Here is the list.

Change in Government policy or legislation wipes out whole companies in a flash.

Change in global economic conditions create huge market change. Just look at the recent banking crisis, the decline of oil prices, etc.

Whole industries have disappeared in the last thirty years. Coal mines, steel mills and the car production plants industry. Nobody saw it coming.

As I type, analysts predict websites will soon be largely redundant due to the growth in mobile apps. Amazing.

Restructuring or delayering of staff in your company as it expands or contracts. That's called progress.

Computer automation and robots, which is one of the fastest growing industries in the world, eliminate the need for people.

Outsourcing of labour to other countries.

Personality clashes with the people you work with.

Geographical change in yours or your partner's work location.

Martians land in London!

The list goes on and on. I am sure you got it. A job for life is nonsense. Get a backup plan or you are going to be in trouble at some point.

Looks pretty grim doesn't it? But hang on, don't reach for the anti-depression pills! Putting your security in a job can be very naive and foolish, that bit is true. However, the same list above presents massive opportunity if your mind is positive, clear and focused on identifying the opportunity in any given situation.

There are great companies out there that need employees with all sorts of skills. If you really want to stand out you have to bring more to the party. Having a great attitude and displaying clear vision are just two of the attributes you will need. This little story is a great example of thinking out of the box.

Two shoe salesman from a huge company land in a remote area of Africa. One of them phones back to head office. "Get me on a plane out of here tomorrow. Nobody wears shoes. We are not going to make any money."

The second salesman phones back to the office. "Boss, you're not going to believe it. Nobody is wearing shoes. We are going to make millions!!"

How you see things conditions your next step. Learn to look for the opportunity.

Myth No. 2: Your job security depends on the company you work for.

The list above proves categorically that you cannot and should not expect a job for life.

Here is a better plan.

Your security depends on you and your ability to produce results in a changing landscape.

All leading universities are very aware of the need for their graduates to develop this skill based mentality. Time and again feedback from industry leaders reflects the changes happening in the work place.

Cross-referencing all the feedback, here are the top five qualities they are looking for:

1. Communication skills: both written and verbal, having a service mentality.

2. Leadership skills: motivation, self-reliance, team building, relationships.

3. Organisation skills: time management, delegation, key performance indicators.

4. Entrepreneurial skills: work ethic, teachable, solution oriented.

5. Big picture thinkers: eyes wide open, stay up-to-date and have a clear understanding of the sector or industry you're in. Have the ability to overcome any obstacle and work towards the end objective, no matter what.

So it's now very clear. If you are serious about becoming an attractive candidate, you have to embrace the desire to develop your skill set. You have to move away from expecting a 'job for life' and focus on developing your 'skills for life'. Develop a set of life skills that will serve you well in any situation, then spend the rest of your life refining and honing these skills until you are the absolute best you can be.

Do that and whatever comes your way, be it change or disruption, it won't matter. You will be an extremely employable person and unlikely to be out of work for long.

Here is an added bonus that you may not recognise now but will become aware of over time. By committing to the process of continuously developing your skills you will become a valuable asset. As a result you are highly likely to be promoted into a position of running the department or business you are in.

So you have the skills. What's your next step?

The very same skills valued by others can be used by you in the development of your own business. Being your own boss and shaping your own destiny for most leaders is the natural next step in their evolution but how do you make the first move?

CHAPTER 2

WHAT IS NETWORK MARKETING AND COULD IT BE YOUR BEST CHANCE TO SUCCEED?

What is Network Marketing and could it be your best chance to succeed?

Imagine if you could find the perfect career and wake up excited about what you do every day. You can and you're about to read about why I believe Network Marketing is your best chance to succeed.

I am fifty years old, I have spent twenty-seven years in Network Marketing and I can honestly say I get up excited and grateful every day. Let me share my passion with you.

Imagine finding a business opportunity you can start part-time alongside your job and develop it to a point where you walk away from work and retire young.

If this is your first exposure to Network Marketing I am happy for you. You are already ahead of the game. This dynamic method of marketing products and services is now being used by many of the world's leading brands. Although it has been around for over sixty years, in the last decade while the world economy has faltered many Network Marketing companies have surged ahead. As people study the concept and understand the reasons for this growth, an increasing band of young professionals are seeing it as an alternative career path.

Here is the simplest way I can describe it.

When a manufacturer produces a product or service they want to take to the marketplace they now have a number of routes available to them. The Network Marketing route, the traditional route and the online route.

The Network Marketing route to market.

In Network Marketing the manufacturer passes the product or service from a warehouse or head office straight to a distribution force of independent, self-employed entrepreneurs who deliver the product or service to their own personal customers they create through their own marketing activity. They then educate the customer on how to get the maximum benefit from the product or service they represent in the hope that it will lead to warm market referrals.

For example, let's say a customer wants to improve their health and appearance and they have heard that consuming a balanced meal replacement shake is a better option to grabbing a sandwich on the run.

They can buy the product off the Internet, they can buy it from a supermarket or they can buy one off a trained Network Marketing distributor who provides them with their own cutting edge exclusive product. In addition to the product supplied the distributor also offers the customer additional materials from the parent company on how to maximise their results.

By contrast I can assure you the manager of the supermarket won't be sending you a text on Monday morning asking how your shake tasted. It's pretty easy to see which one is the better service for the customer. So let's look at how you create income in Network Marketing.

The manufacturer does not have to pay the overheads of employing a large work-force and all the associated capital costs relating to the distribution of the product or service. This represents a considerable saving.

Let's look at how that saving is distributed as an income to the self-employed, independent Network Marketing distributor salesforce.

Income stream 1 – Retail:

The Distributor (sometimes called Member or Business Owner) generates an income from the retail sales they make to their own customers.

Income stream 2 – Royalty:

The Distributor can create a royalty based income by introducing and training new distributors to create and look after their own customers. The turnover created is tracked by the parent company and you are paid a small percentage royalty commission based on the sales volume of your team.

The most successful companies focus on outstanding customer service. There is no commission paid for introducing new distributors. Income is only generated when product is purchased through outstanding service to personal customers and customers being looked after by someone in your team.

When the product or service creates a result or benefit for the customer, the customer is happy to refer you to other customers and the holy grail of business is achieved: 'the warm market referral'.

Let's compare that model with the changes happening to the simple traditional business model and the emergence of the online business model.

The traditional route to market.

The manufacturer creates a product or service, they pass it to a super wholesaler, they pass to a wholesaler, they pass to a retailer and the retailer delivers the product or service to the customer.

In recent times one of the difficulties for the traditional model has been the escalating costs associated with getting the product or service to the end customer. Wages, rents, rates and many other expenses are all increasing while profit margins continue to get squeezed by the online giants like Amazon etc.

Many of these operations based on the high streets are disappearing fast and with them go millions of jobs. For now, the ones that survive are forced to sell increasing quantities of products or service just to cover their costs. The time available for real customer education and care on how to use the product or service is extremely limited.

Many of these companies are now having to rethink their strategy and are in serious transition. Their business model is caught between the traditional and the online model. They recognise the need for customer support and education but realise the front line retailer has limited resource. The answer for the bigger operations with sufficient resource has been to create centralised online customer care facilities and improved web content. These facilities will never be as good as local support and education but it's their only hope.

The online model is here to stay.

In recent years we have seen an explosion in online retailing supported by next day delivery. People have become comfortable surfing the net for exactly what they need. They can access product information at the click of a mouse and compare the best prices from across the globe in a Nano second. These operations are changing the way we shop and the way we think about shopping and they are here to stay.

Let's look at just a few examples from the last twelve months.

Building a new house:

The building game is not one of the first industries that would spring to mind when it comes to online sales. We have access to a number of excellent building supply merchants locally and naturally used them for many things. The biggest change the Internet allowed us to do was instantly get prices and quotes from every single element of the build. This saved us thousands of pounds and cut the margin of profit the local merchant would have made if we were naive.

As well as help us with the day to day items needed it also allowed us to research the very latest building methods and products that were not available locally.

Do not underestimate the impact of the online model.

Tony's story:

Tony sells shoes. He buys wholesale lots and then sells the individual pieces to the public via a number of high street shops and attends weekly market stall events. He recently observed the growth of online Internet sales for a wide range of items and realised he could do the same. After some research he wisely hired some young staff who have steered him into creating an efficient online presence. Over the last year he has gone from a declining business model selling forty or fifty pairs of shoes per day to a booming business with over five hundred sales per day and is heading towards a thousand pairs per day.

It's a great example of an old dog (sorry Tony) learning new skills and I could not be happier for him.

Just like the growth of social media platforms, online retailing is yet another example of how quickly the landscape can and does change. These changes are here to stay. If businesses don't adapt they will die.

Leading Network Marketing companies are able to embrace change and stay ahead of trends.

Today the leading Network Marketing companies offer the perfect mix of traditional customer care practices through their local distributor base, combined with cutting edge online communication and support.

In Network Marketing the profit margins and costs consumed by the super wholesaler, wholesaler and retailers are saved and redirected to pay the distributors' income streams 1 and 2 as explained above.

Using this simple structure of income generation, millions of people all over the world are creating levels of financial independence that would have been impossible on a normal career path.

It amazes me how few people know about the opportunity offered by Network Marketing. It's still one of the world's best kept secrets. People from all walks of life have stumbled upon it but main stream society are largely unaware of the career option it offers them.

If you have an ambition to live an above average life, I assure you it will be worth every minute you put into it. In the next chapter I am going to share my story with you. Although it's been a rollercoaster of a ride it's hard to believe the level of success that has come my way just based on the lessons laid out in this book. I could have written hundreds of pages so I hope you enjoy just a few of the bits I have left in.

CHAPTER 3

MY STORY. IT'S BEEN A ROLLERCOASTER RIDE. IF I CAN DO IT, SO CAN YOU.

My story. It's been a rollercoaster ride. If I can do it, so can you.

I was born in November 1964 in Port Talbot, South Wales. I have two sisters and one brother. I am the youngest so have always been known as the baby of the family. My eldest sister Karen has been a huge inspiration since my very first memories. A superb artist and singer. My other sister Dawn is one of the kindest, hardworking ladies I have ever known and my brother Barrie, who beat me from a young age. Err sorry, taught me self defence! He is a big heart on legs, one of my best friends and has always looked out for me.

Mum and dad. What can I say? Dad died five years ago and I miss him every day. I had no idea how much losing him would mean to me then and now, Although we had great days, just like many other people, I feel I lost him before being able to share the good times we now have. He was a great guy and no doubt I will make reference to him a lot in this book. Mum, best described by my Uncle Arnold (Dad's brother) as superwoman. She never complains about anything and has a great sense of humour. Every time her two metal knee caps light up the airport security machines and she gets patted down, it's a chance for her to have fun, chat up the guards and bring a little sunshine into their mundane jobs. Inspiration.

The early years

I came from a normal working class background. Dad worked as an electrician for a local engineering company and rose through the ranks in the local steelworks to be in charge of over a hundred men. Mum worked in the local fish and chip shop and was a cleaner at our school. Pretty much everyone I knew lived in the same or similar houses and everyone learned to help each other in any way they could. In those days, of the fifty-six houses in the street I could pretty much name every single person in every house. Times have changed now. People send an email to their neighbors instead of crossing the road. I think some people call that progress. I am not so sure. Change is a theme I will come back to later. Few things ever stay the same but hanging onto some old-fashioned values will serve you well.

The very first job I remember having was around the age of nine, riding the milk delivery floats. If you are reading this and wondering what a milk delivery float was, let me enlighten you. Before the major supermarkets took over the universe milk was delivered directly to people's door in the early hours of every morning.

My heroes weren't people like Steve Jobs, Jeff Besos, or Richard Branson. It was Dai the milkman who carried four glass pint bottles in each hand and still had time to close Mrs. Jenkins's gate behind him. Giants of men who still make me smile today.

I also remember when orange juice became available to order. The rich people in our streets were easy to identify. No not the Range Rover on the drive. It was the fresh orange juice that gave them away.

It wasn't long before I realised delivering papers was more profitable. I bought a delivery round off a teenager who had grown up and my new enterprise was born. Pretty soon a few more teenagers had graduated onto cleaning cars, allowing my empire to grow to three rounds, two of which I rented out for a small fee. Without knowing it the seeds of entrepreneurship were born.

The teenage years

Also, around this age I discovered I was talented at drawing pretty much anything. So portrait painting become a real bread winner for me. Even today people remind me they still have pictures I painted of their pets almost forty years ago. Pretty cool.

In these early years, I realised a big smile and a great attitude usually led to more tips, whether it was milk papers or portraits. One of the many customer service lessons I had no idea I was learning at the time. Over the next few years I became consumed by my art and knew I had found my love affair for life. That's another thing I will come back to.

In 1984 the Conservative government led by Margaret Thatcher was on a collision course with the miners unions. These were challenging and uncertain days for families in heavy industry. So with a heavy heart I quit school, gave up my passion for art and took the safe route of making money as an apprentice electrician.

I have no interest in the rights or wrongs of this time but I do have deep and painful memories that will stay with me forever. I remember the picket lines where the coal lorries ran the gauntlet to keep the steelworks running. I remember my dad going to work in London because he would not cross the picket line. I remember policemen taunting the miners with how much money they were making while the miners relied on hand-outs and food parcels. I remember the fathers and sons fighting in the local bars over whether to cross the picket line. These were dark days and many families never recovered.

Without knowing it at the time, here is what it taught me: I did not want to be trapped and manipulated. I needed to get out. It was time to grow up. Between ages sixteen and nineteen I really started to study and realised if I kept getting distinctions at college the company I worked for would keep paying for my education.

Still an apprentice and living at home, life was pretty safe and simple but all this was about to change overnight. At age nineteen the steel industry was in real trouble. My dad was my boss in the firm I was working for. He called me into the office one day and said: "I am sorry son. We have no work for you, so I have to let you go". My dad was a proud man and never showed weakness easily. It was twenty-six years later as I helped nurse him through the final days of his life that I found out he cried that night, feeling he had let me down. Waw, this is getting tough to type!

(Whiskey break).

Ok. I feel better now. I'm sure Dad will look down and have a chuckle as I type the next bit.

The summer of '84. Tap dancing on the wing of a plane as it taxies down the run way and team meetings in pole dancing bars in Canada

So here is what else happened that summer. The next bit is pretty crazy but trust me I have the newspaper clippings and TV newsreels to prove it. Rugby was by now a huge part of my life and the end of season tour was upon us. I flew to Jersey with Taibach RFC for our centenary tour celebrations. We boarded the plane in Cardiff. Maybe the captain could have spotted there were going to be a few issues as we literally carried some of the team onto the plane. But hey, these were the days before health and safety ran the world and we managed to take off.

As the plane touched down the emergency door adjacent to the row I was in was missing. Now I am no an aircraft engineer but I can feel a draft when it's nearby. Someone had opened the door on landing and it was now out on the wing.

It's amazing how fast you sober up when something goes wrong. I thought waw, that's not good. So I tried to reach out for the door. As quick as a flash my friends saw an opportunity and launched me out onto the wing. Realising they were not going to let me back in (and please do not ask me why I did what I am about to say) I thought hey, let's enjoy the moment. So I started tap dancing along the wing. Just like any normal person would do right? The propellers just feet away whizzed around in a blur ready to chop me into little bits if I made one wrong move.

The army had been called prior to us arriving. I am on every TV channel and in every national newspaper. I got taken straight to jail. Needless to say, when I got home I was banned for life from playing rugby in Wales and my world had fallen apart.

Although I put on a brave face, this was the single biggest blow I had ever dealt with at that point in my life. It's tough to explain. Rugby truly was my school, church and home all in one place and in a flash it was gone.

Although I was banned from playing for Welsh Rugby Union teams there is another union called the Welsh Junior Union and thankfully I was able to play for a team called Pontrhydyfen, birthplace of Richard Burton and Ivor Emanuel. It's a fantastic little Welsh mining village and they embraced me with open arms.

After my very first training session I met my lifelong friends Gareth and Christine Jenkins. Gareth and Chris would often put me up overnight as my new club was a long way from my home. Gareth and Chris had spent the previous summer season in Canada and would talk into the night about the amazing time they had. They told me I would be crazy not to go and play there and they were looking for player coaches. The thought of barbecues and hot tub parties was too much and within a few months I was off.

That summer went by in a blur, playing rugby with men who had fingers bigger than my legs, team meetings in pole dancing bars and steaks the size of coffee tables.

If you have seen the movie American Pie you will get the idea so enough said.

I did not realise how much my vision of life had changed until I came back to the UK. So there was no way I could stay in Port Talbot. My brother managed to get me a job as an electrician in London and within a few weeks I was off again. I was a terrible electrician, always dreaming of things and not getting much done. Thankfully my qualifications were about to serve me well.

After an inauspicious start I was quickly sent to head office in Birmingham where they were looking to train young engineers to join the management team. This was a huge break at such a young age and I remember Mum and Dad were so proud.

Over the next two years I worked long hours commuting back and forth between London, Wales and Birmingham and was totally committed to my career.

Although I worked with a fantastic group of people and loved my job, deep down I knew it was not what I wanted. No matter how hard I tried there was something missing. I could not see myself going back and forth every day for the rest of my life to the same office no matter what they paid me. Canada was playing on my mind more and more each day and I knew I had to go back.

If you ever have felt this way, it probably indicates that you have a passion for being an entrepreneur. Hold on to these feelings. It's your inner voice trying to break through.

Meeting Deb.

On one of my weekend trips home I met Deb in Neath. Although she was on a date with a friend of mine Andrew I knew she was the one. She was different to everyone else. Huge eyes, big hair and the warmest personality I had ever met. Being the skilled business coach that I am, I went with my instincts. I threw her over my shoulder and ran up the street with her. After being pounded on the head a few times I put her down. She hated me but I told her there and then that I was going to marry her. She thought I was crazy but over the following weeks we became great friends. Some things are just meant to be and we have been together ever since. I promised to keep this short so I will give you the full-blown Mills and Boon version in another book.

Although Deb and I had grown very close and knew we had something special, I was still very much a free spirit and knew I had to spread my wings.

Canada, Hawaii, Fiji and finally Australia.

The summer season was about to begin and it was time for me to leave. Deb and I played it cool and agreed to keep in touch using letters and the personal ads in papers, just like Madonna and Sean Penn did in the movie Desperately Seeking Susan. No mobile phones, email or Facebook in those days. More on that in the next book. Kisses and hugs on the platform, a strong hand shake from my dad and the train pulled out of Port Talbot train station. This was going to be a long trip so there was no shortage of tears. Waw, this is really taking me back. I feel another whiskey moment coming on. Give me a minute. Ok. Better now.

Canada was amazing. Huge expanses of land. Everything was enormous. The people, the mountains, the moon, the northern lights. I could go on and on. Looking back I was just a kid and I was learning so much without even knowing it.

As you read this, make a personal note to travel the world and see it all. Trust me, no job is worth missing out on the wonders of life. Whatever they pay, it's not enough!

Just so you are aware, I know you have picked up this book to learn about business and may be wondering when I am going to get to the good stuff. In time you will realise success is not a destination, it's a journey. Business is all about knowing why you want to succeed. The how to get there is a walk in the park for the people who take a little time understanding what they want.

Hawaii was, well, Hawaii. The scent in the air, the gentle breeze. It's magical and you have to go there, it's truly breathtaking. Fiji. Hey, if you don't like walking on miles of white sandy beaches framed by turquoise oceans with dolphins leaping to greet you, then don't go! Obviously I could write and write about the times I had there. What I want you to do is just promise me you're not going to waste your life. There is so much to see and I want you to see it all.

Finally, I get to Sydney Australia. Undoubtedly one of the most incredible city ports in the world. My head is spinning. Close the book, click on Google images and spend thirty minutes looking at the pictures and videos of Canada, Hawaii, Fiji and Australia. If you know why you want to succeed, when the right opportunity comes along those images will be the petrol on your fire. Travel made me realise that there is so much to see. It's a bit like having a big bumble bee in your arse! You just won't be able to sit down. Once you get your dream clear in your head you will know exactly what I mean! Get yourself a big bumble bee and motivation will not be an issue.

Landing in Sydney I headed straight for Drumoyne Rugby club, a team my friend Richard had played for the year before. The boys there allowed me to crash at their house and helped me get my bearings. Team sports are amazing. Overnight I had a group of friends and was ready to go. I needed work fast as there was only two hundred and fifty pounds left in my account.

I went for a few interviews and with the lessons learned from those early years I put on a big smile and managed to blag myself a great job working as an electrical design engineer. On day one I arrived one hour early and left one hour late. All that week I made it my ambition to let my willingness to work and help stand out and it worked. Totally skint and down to my last pennies I asked the boss for an advance on my wages and he agreed.

By the way, back in Wales Deb had itchy feet and also jacked in a safe job with Nat West (truth is she was missing me) and was on her way to Australia with her friend Nicola. By the time they arrived I was set up in my own apartment and life was amazing.

Learning how to build a royalty income was a bombshell moment.

Then came the day that changed my life. And I mean changed my life, so concentrate on the next bit. Tanya was a lovely young lady and worked as an engineer with me. Totally trustworthy and very unassuming, she was the sort of person you'd want to baby-sit your kids.

As much as I loved my new job (and I did) I would look out the window and see people sailing across the harbour on a weekday afternoon. I was dreaming. Waw, imagine how lucky they must feel with all that freedom and to be out of the rat race.

Then one day, she walked up to me and said: "Jeff, I went to a business meeting last night and saw a presentation that was amazing. It's not for me but I know you are going to do it! Here is the guy's card. Please give him a call."

I said: "What's it about?" She said: "You need to call him and take a look." Great answer! That night I called the number. "Hi, my name is Jeff Williams. A friend of mine Tanya said I need to call you and take a look at what you are doing."

The following night we took the ferry, train and then bus for two hours to get to the other side of the city. We had no idea what we were going to see but Tanya said we should go, so we did.

That was the night I first set eyes on the business concept that this book is dedicated to, namely Network Marketing. The presentation blew me away. I got it instantly and have been in love with what I do ever since. In a flash everything I wanted from life was available at my finger tips and the only person in the world who could stop me achieving whatever I wanted in life was me. I felt like I had won the lottery ten times over! Here are the lines that got me:

"Imagine if you could be time and money rich. What would you do with your life?"

"Imagine if you could find a business which, once built properly, would return you a royalty based income allowing you to do whatever you want."

My mind and heart was racing. Remember those pictures I just told you to look at? Remember me giving up my passion for being an artist to go and work as an electrician because it paid the bills? Based on what I had seen there was so much more I wanted to do. I was in. Not only was I in, I did not care what it was I was in to. Seriously, when you are at a point of knowing you will do whatever it takes to create the life you want you are half way there.

I went home buzzing with ideas about how fast I was going to build my empire. Freedom was always my driver. Imagine building a business where nobody pulled your chain. You could do what you want when you wanted. I could not stop talking about it.

The timing was perfect. Our visas were about to expire so we agreed we would start as soon as we got back to the UK.

The coach crash in New Zealand and the lessons learned.

A few days later we flew to New Zealand to watch the Commonwealth Games. While touring around the South Island we decided to book a trip to Milford Sounds and then to do the biggest bungee jump in the world at the time, on the way back to our hostel in Queenstown. The Milford Sounds rocked my world. While travelling I kept a journal, something I recommend everyone should do. At the end of each day I would jot down a few lines to record my thoughts and feelings about what I was experiencing. On this day this is what I wrote:

"This was the greatest day of my life."

I had never made that entry before and have never made it since.

The following day as our bus came out of the Homer tunnel we slowed to let a bus pass on our inside. We were in seat numbers fourteen and fifteen. As we crept forward I shouted to the driver: "HEY DRIVER, WE ARE REALLY CLOSE TO THE EDGE!" No sooner had I shouted those words, the rear wheels slipped off the gravel shoulder. The front wheels followed and the bus lurched forty-five degrees. I looked at Deb and said: "Hang on babe, we are going over."

There were thirty-six of us in the bus at the top and six left in the bus at the bottom. The bus rolled six times. Each one felt like slow motion and one by one we watched our friends smash through the windows. When the bus settled at the bottom of the valley in a riverbed it was like a scene from Apocalypse Now. Bodies strewn everywhere, blood spraying from head wounds, compound fractures jutting out of legs, it was total carnage. Inside the bus you could not see a thing. I reached out for Deb but she was gone. A few seconds later I heard her. "Jeff!" she cried, "Jeff!" She was ok.

Seat number sixteen was taken by a guy who decided last minute to ride down the mountain with us. To this day I have no idea why. He had cycled all the way to the top and it was downhill from there. He wasn't moving. After getting Deb out I climbed back in the bus to see who was left. As I pulled on his legs to get him out I realised he was dead. He was crushed and there was nothing I could do.

Pretty soon a small army was scrambling down the mountain and helicopters landed close by. A young doctor made a lifesaving decision that day. He looked at me and somehow realised that something was wrong and decided I may be bleeding internally. Although I had no obvious external injuries I was really struggling to breathe and my lips were blue. He gave me a space on the helicopter which, as it turned out, saved my life. Forty-five minutes later, slipping in and out of a coma I arrived at Invercargill hospital's intensive care unit.

I had a ruptured spleen, multiple lacerations to liver and kidneys and lower basal collapse in my right lung. I was a mess and hanging by a thread. There was no room in the helicopter for Deb. She had to endure an agonising three hour drive before arriving at my bedside. The signs were not good.

I was given only hours to live. I was bleeding internally. They knew if it did not stop soon they would have to operate and could not offer odds of more than fifty-fifty. Thankfully the bleeding did stop and little by little I started to stabilise, thanks to the efforts of an amazing team.

The speed at which you lose muscle in intensive care is rapid. Having a nurse bed bath you, then hoist you onto a commode strips away your male ego pretty quick. Graduating from a wheelchair to a Zimmer frame was a big day. So many valuable lessons were carried forward with me from the bus crash. You just never know what tomorrow holds. We all need each other and so much more. I said to Deb: "Hey if I can get through this, building that business will be a piece of cake."

Our first attempt at Network Marketing.

We decided to go over land through Indonesia, Malaysia, Thailand, Hong Kong, China, Mongolia, Russia, Poland and Germany. We eventually made it home. It was time to start a new life.

Within a few weeks we found out that our postman was involved in the same company we had seen in Australia. I could not believe our luck and neither could he. We barely had a penny behind us but we were filled with ambition.

We were excited and we were laser beam focused. Well that's what we thought at the time. Looking back I was a complete amateur to be honest but hey, the naivety of youth is a common state of mind. During the daytime I worked as a portrait artist. The accident reminded me of who I wanted to be. Deb worked as an office temp. We were skint but I was giving Deb the big promise that we were destined for the top and the truth is I believed it.

We were flat-out, chasing the dream and there was no room for doubt. Within a few years we had become rising stars and qualified for the free company holidays held in various glamorous locations. Although we were not making big money we felt we were within touching distance of making it to the big time. I proposed to Deb, we got married and started to plan our life on easy street.

Over the next five years, now with a young baby on board, I kept pushing but could never regain the momentum I initially created. If I had this book in my hand at the time it would have been a totally different story and that's why I wanted to write it. After a total of seven years I was burnt out and my business was in freefall. I had to accept defeat and go get a job in the local steelworks.

I was crushed and our relationship was seriously tested.

My first taste of failure in business. The wilderness years. Reflection and learning.

Earlier-on I wrote how devastated I was at having my rugby legs 'chopped off'. Then the bus accident pushed me right to the brink. Let me be honest with you, that was nothing compared to seeing your dream in tatters, watching hope evaporate and seeing your wife look at you as a loser. Now that, my friend, sucks.

Sitting in the steelworks canteen was a whole lot different to going to work on a ferry in Sydney. Most of the guys I worked with were great and talked about rugby life etc. but thankfully (and I mean thankfully) there were a few who could not wait to taunt me. I hope you have a few in your life. Every day they took great pleasure in saying things like "The globetrotter returns!" "You're never going to get out of here!" They thought it was funny. I clearly remember sitting in the steelworks canteen, reading Think and Grow Rich by Napoleon Hill and The Magic of Thinking Big by Doctor David Swartz, just to keep my dreams alive and listening to the boys relentlessly take the mickey.

The bottom line was that I had failed because I lacked all the tools to succeed and it was time to do some soul searching. No matter how hard I tried I just could not quit on chasing the dream. Deb was great. Never complaining, just getting by, day-by-day but inside my guts were churning like a cement mixer.

Around this time I had a call from my old friend who had just got started in a company based in L.A. He was so excited. Remember how I described myself earlier in the story? David was just as excited! The timing was not right, I felt totally beaten up, so I shot him down in flames in that first call and he dropped the phone with scorch marks on his ear. Over the next few years he called a few more times and then eventually after two years he called and said Jeff, I have just come back from a major event, business is flying and you would be stupid not to at least take a look. He had changed and I knew he was going to succeed with or without me.

My second attempt at Network Marketing. Older, wiser and ready to smash it.

That weekend I made the long drive to Dover where my mate David was living. I drove there in my two tone Volkswagen Polo. It was white and rust, worth four hundred and fifty pounds, it had no radio or heater and I talked to it all the way. "Come on baby, you're doing great, you can make it." Broke people reading this will know what I mean. I was praying we would get there and back.

Although I had spent seven years with the biggest Network Marketing company in the world, what I did not realise (probably because I was having a prolonged bought of stupidity) was that not all companies have the same compensation plan. When you think about it, it's pretty obvious. Certain products allow greater margins than others, allowing the company to offer greater rewards for a similar amount of work.

If the truth be known, Dave was nowhere near as professional looking as the guys we used to work with. They all looked sharp. Dave sat there looking like a cross between a WWF fighter and a New age camp site leader. Pony tail, big earrings, striped baggy pants. You just can't make this stuff up. Classic. Laughing as I type, he is going to kill me for that.

Dave was street smart. At age sixteen we used to work together in the steel-works listening to Bruce Springsteen songs about breaking free. He knew I had dreams. He knew deep inside me there was a burning inferno and he knew how to light it. He remembered the payphone conversation that scorched his ears. His posture was perfect. He wasn't trying to sell me any-thing. In fact, thinking about it (and I have never said this to him) he was world class and he got my attention, big time.

Here is what he did. He knew I wasn't the most patient guy in the world so he didn't waffle. He knew if I was going to do it, it would be based on the ev-idence he provided me and not a fancy speech. He showed me the products and allowed me to try them. Then within seconds and while I was tasting the products he played me all the answer machine messages he had stored of clients wanting to buy them, message after message after message. "Hi Dave. It's Claire. I feel amazing! Can I buy some more?" "Hi Dave. It's Karen. Waw, I cannot tell you how great I feel. My friend wants some product too. When can we come around?" etc.

He then showed me pictures of the results his customers were getting. Sci-entists tell us that people absorb information in four different ways:

1. Physically: touch, taste, smell.

2. Audibly: hearing something.

3. Visually: seeing something.

4. Spiritually: feeling something.

He looked at me, smiled a knowing smile, drew the simplest marketing plan explanation I had ever seen and he knew he had knocked it out of the park. I was in!

This was my second chance and I was not going to blow it. Deb was dead against it but there was no other option for me. I was not going to let myself rot in the steelworks. Within a few months she came around and together over the next three years we totally committed to getting to the top. Nothing was going to stop me. I was taking no prisoners and carrying no baggage. I learned as fast as I could, studied what all the successful distributors were doing and copied their every move. I went from making a thousand pounds per month to making over twenty thousand pounds per month and I was on top of the world.

These were great days. Dave found himself a soulmate in Jane. He had also brought in Tony and Gerry and I had brought in Mark and Anita. We had all grown up together in the steelworks (not the girls) and we marched forward together all the way to the top of the company. I finished in the steelworks, bought Deb's mum a house, bought my mum and dad's house off them so they could have the cash tied up in it released to enjoy their retirement, put the kids into a great school, bought our dream home (a barn conversion near the ocean) and bought Deb a brand new Porsche. Life was amazing. At age thirty-six, finally the dream was real.

Losing our leader.

May 21st 2000, 3 o'clock in the afternoon, Deb calls me. She cannot stop crying and cannot get her words out. "Take your time babe, I can't understand you. Take a deep breath." She was sobbing uncontrollably. Then I heard the words: "Mark's dead! Mark's dead Jeff!" "What do you mean Deb? Which Mark?" "Mark Hughes! David has just called me crying. Mark's dead." Waw, this is tough to type. He was such a great guy. All over the world there are people who miss him so much and I am one of them.

Mark Hughes was the most charismatic man I had ever met. He was the founder leader and number one distributor in the company. He was funny, dynamic, good looking, passionate and caring. He was amazing and now he was gone.

With Mark gone, many people lost their talisman. The flag bearer that we all happily rallied around was no longer with us. The hole he left was impossible to fill and despite everyone's best efforts the company struggled in the years that followed.

Although they were tough times, I still thought our business would just go from strength to strength such was our confidence at the time. For a number of years it did but eventually the clouds gathered and we were about to be tested yet again. There was so much going on. Lots of people had different ideas on the best way to proceed and confusion set in. I lost my focus and if you want to get paid like a leader, focus is everything. I stopped doing the things that built our business in the first place, started to manage instead of lead and as a result once again our growth stalled and then started to slide backwards. When I look back I was stupid and should have known better but hindsight is a wonderful thing.

Starting a new life in Spain.

Time marches on. By now Georgia was twelve and Joshua was eight. We were right in the middle of one of the wettest periods ever recorded in Wales. It had rained almost every day for two months. The business had lost its sparkle and we needed to do something to ignite the dream because our flame was fading away. Deb and I chatted late into the night and both realised we needed a break from the UK. Our life in Australia was still vivid in our minds and we desperately needed some sun. We knew we could run our business from anywhere in the world, so after lots of research and a few field trips we opted to move to Marbella in Southern Spain.

The kids would learn to speak Spanish and French in their International school and we were able to check out other ways of building our business.

During this time our UK based business continued to slide. They were difficult days for everyone. We knew we had to find a way of reversing this trend or we were in trouble. As we lived in Spain we were able to mix with both the expat English community and the Spanish and Latin American leaders. Everyone was so kind and generous and we will be forever grateful.

The kids settled into their new school. Deb enjoyed ironing in the sun. We played tennis and golf as a family and for the second time ever my skin managed to go from white to a golden cream colour. I think some people call it pink. Anyway, back to business.

Although I did not speak Spanish I could see the Latin American community were flying and I needed to understand what was going on. I had a chance to go to a leadership event in Granada, Spain, so packed my bags. From memory there were a thousand Spanish, about five hundred Portuguese and a speaker from Venezuela who was amazing, totally excited and laser focused. I loved it. Everyone was so passionate. It reminded me of how I used to feel.

A colleague of mine kindly translated the main points and once again I could feel the fire rise within me.

Finding our way back.

I learned enough at the Granada event to know I needed to find out more. I contacted colleagues of mine in the States and asked them to help arrange tours to areas of the world that were growing the fastest. Whilst it was exciting to know Latin America was doing so well, we all felt that their culture was not a close enough match for our mainly UK and Ireland based operation. So they suggested Texas and Iceland as better options as they too were also doing great.

We contacted all of our key leaders in the UK and Ireland and told them that we needed to find a way forward and explained our plan. We paid for a group to go to Texas and took a group to Iceland. The trips were a revelation. We all learned so much and a small core of our leaders once more felt they had a clear plan for growth. When we got back we were different to everyone else. We had seen firsthand where the company was going and there was no way we were going to be left behind.

The perfect storm.

Despite the decline we had been through, confidence was returning to the team so it was time to ramp things up. In March 2011 we asked our whole organisation if they wanted to come with us to California to take another look at the areas growing the fastest. We had seen the impact it made on the ones who had gone on the previous trip and knew we needed to expose more of them to what was going on. This time though they had to pay their own way as we were looking for the next band of leaders. Twenty-eight people decided to come.

The trip was amazing and will stay with all of us forever. We hired two huge minibuses and drove all over California. You just had to be there.

At the end of the tour Deb and I joined the rest of the top leaders of the company for our annual event. All companies go through evolutions and we are no different. What I saw at the event was the birth of a brand new company. The transition was complete. The new CEO and his team had got our company into the best shape it's ever been in and we had a small team ready to rock and roll.

We all came home and killed it. Over the next four years our turnover went from a hundred thousand per month to one million per month. Our income explodes and our team are on fire.

We are now laser beam focused on where we are going. We are helping lots of young people (many straight out of university) use social media to communicate our company's message and cannot wait to see what the next twenty years brings.

Although it's been a long and difficult path it's been worth every step. Of course, there have been many times we questioned ourselves but we knew we had to keep pushing on.

We are now living back in Wales. We have just built a beautiful eight thousand square feet home in a great location. Both kids have benefited from watching us fight our way through and as a result have learned the value of hard work. They are fun to be around, extremely well grounded and for that I am very grateful. Georgia had the best results in her school and is now doing a double honours in Spanish and French at Bristol University. Joshua is following right behind her.

None of us can know what the future holds. The rest of this book is all about the lessons we learned along the way. As you read, please remember I am not a writer. The grammar and punctuation won't be perfect, so try and forgive me.

I am just going to pour out all I have with the hope that it helps you make sense of the crazy world we live in. Life is rarely perfect and it's going to take a ton of courage to get to wherever you want to go but for me it's been worth every single step.

CHAPTER 4

LESSONS FROM THE COALFACE. THE QUALITIES YOU WILL NEED TO SUCCEED.

Lessons from the coalface. The qualities you will need to succeed

Rather than assume that you understand that title, let's look into it and add a little heartfelt emotion to understand what it really means. The coalface was the most dangerous job in the mining industry. Working in tight little tunnels miles underground that could collapse at any moment. Boys as young as twelve years of age would work alongside men for twelve hours a day, crawling around, digging out coal in hot, stifling conditions with nothing more than their bare hands and a few tools.

When we contemplate the work we need to do to succeed, let's keep everything in perspective. Compared to what other people have had to do to survive in life, learning to build a business should be a walk in the park.

The miners were not paid for the words they spoke, they were paid for the coal they dug out of the ground. This chapter is about the qualities you will need to make it in life, plain and simple. Only the miners who worked in those conditions and felt the helplessness of being underground can ever relate to each other's fears and anxieties. It's the same in business because I have personally felt the pain, the anxiety, the doubt and then the elation of breaking through and succeeding. I am confident I can reach out to you and set you on a path that will serve you well, whatever your starting position is. If you want to make it in life you have got to be prepared to give it all you've got. Before we get started, here is a classic story that illustrates this point perfectly.

It's about a young boy who asked an old man what the secret to success was.

The old man had a reassuring nature and the young boy felt safe that he would guide him to the truth. "Take my hand", he said, "Let's go for a walk as we chat." The old man led him down to the ocean and started to walk in. The young boy hesitated and said: "Where are we going?" "Don't worry", said the old man, "Just hold onto my hand." Pretty soon the water was lapping around the boys chin. "I can't swim", he said, "I am getting a little scared." The old man's expression changed as he looked down on the boy, then in a flash the old man released his hand and placed both of his big hands on the boy's head and pushed him under the water.

At first the boy thought it was just a game as he knew the old man was trusted by everyone in his town, so he tried to relax and hold his breath. After a little while he needed to breathe, so he started to push up with his head but the old man was stronger and he pushed down. Panic started to set in and the boy pushed as hard as he could but the old man was much stronger. Gasping for air and about to drown the boy gave it one last try. He summoned up every bit of energy he had and pushed up with every ounce of his tiny frame.

Lying on the beach, spitting water onto the sand, the young boy's vision slowly came back. In front of him he could see the smiling face of the old man. "You nearly killed me!" he cried, "You are a mad man! Why did you do this to me?"

"Dear child. You were in no danger and I would never hurt you. You asked me to teach you the secret to success. Let me ask you a question. When you thought you were going to drown, how badly did you want to feel the fresh air in your lungs? And how hard did you push to break through the surface?"

The young boy paused then said: "I wanted to breathe so badly I was scared and I knew I would die if I didn't push with everything I had."

The old man replied: "When you want to succeed as badly as you want to breathe, then and only then will you be successful."

I love that story and you may well have heard it a few times. I make no apology for rolling it out one more time. It's so simple and so true. Keep it in mind as we go forward.

The Magnificent 7.

So what are the big keys to leading a successful life and getting out of the rat race? I call these 'The Magnificent Seven'.

You can apply these to anything you choose to do. Tested across thousands of different disciplines and cultures, use them as your foundation for whatever you pursue. Again this is me trying to keep it simple. There are many great books that will elaborate further but hopefully this clear-cut version will get you started. Here is the list then I will add an explanation to each one.

1. Attitude: have a great attitude no matter what.

2. Ambition: nothing ever happens without ambition.

3. Vision: for what is possible in your life.

4. Belief: without it you are paralysed.

5. Confidence: people who lack belief need your confidence, it's as simple as that.

6. Action: without it the above are just words.

7. Evaluate: keep getting better and you are destined for success.

(Reflection break).

I just realised I had better drop this in here because I know what's coming up. Although I have shared my story, albeit as briefly as I could, we don't know each other and I am a total stranger at this point. Because we have not met and you are not looking into my eyes, it's hard for me to convey the compassion, hope and enthusiasm I hold for you and anyone else who wants to do something with their life. It's hard for me to get you to believe that I understand being confused, scared, frustrated or any other emotion that may be holding you back.

Picture yourself sitting opposite me. Picture us as having been good friends for a long time and I am someone you can trust. Take a moment to think about that. Go on, picture it if you can. Here is all I know. If you can grow to trust what I write as advice you can follow, then this book will help. If you can't, it won't. For some it will help a little, for others it will re-shape their life. But if there is no trust, there is no relationship and none of this will work. I hope that resonates a little, it's really important.

We are all so different. Debbie is totally different to me. Give her a Danielle Steele novel and she is lost in a world of romantic bliss, crying and smiling. She is in heaven. I prefer things to be gritty and real. I don't need things dressed in bows. I like life the way it is. With that in mind, the text that follows is going to be hard-hitting and straight to the point. If I had to I can do the fluffy stuff. The problem is, that approach has never worked that well for me. Hopefully we are now on the same page so let's get started.

1. Attitude.

You're going to need a great attitude about everything all the time, no matter what. It's as simple as that. I could stop typing there but let me expand it a little just in case you need more of an understanding.

When the sky falls in (and it will) your attitude will dictate your behaviour. If you want to be seen as a successful person it needs to be something like this: "Careful, the sky is falling in. Let's move over here so we are out of the way." As opposed to: "AAAHHH! THE SKY IS FALLING IN! RRRUUNNNN!" Successful people are calm in the face of any crisis. Learn not to panic. Pause, breathe, think and act. It will serve you well.

It's pointless me dressing up the next line.

Keep everything in perspective. I see people all the time caught up in what they believe to be a major drama. Come on, wake up. While you sit there and learn how to develop yourself and your skills, there is someone on the other side of the world starving to death wondering how they will feed their kids today. It's so easy to get caught up in what we believe to be major issues in our lives. They are not major at all but you need something to scale them against, so let me try and help.

Here is one of mine. I hope it helps.

Remember my story of me lying in bed clinging to life? Guess what? There were two beds in the intensive care unit. I was in one and there was a six week old baby in the other one. Her family had been in a head-on collision. The mother was holding her in her arms and the baby was not strapped in. The baby was catapulted through the window. Each day, just a few feet away, I watched the family weep and beg for her to survive. She didn't make it.

Heart-wrenching stuff like that happens every day. Let it get your attention. Let life touch you. Don't be so busy caught up in the drama of your own issues believing you're the world's only victim. Look around. Life can get a whole lot tougher, so here is a polite request: get over yourself. As I lay there and watched that tragedy unfold I realised I was the lucky one and that helped me with my own crisis. From then on I made myself a promise. My attitude would be 'no problem' to everything that came my way. Try those two words the next time your attitude is tested: "no problem". Life is just a series of tests. Your attitude in advance of each test will make a huge impact on the outcome.

Don't underestimate the value in applying that rule to pretty much everything that comes your way. Learn to diminish the size of your perceived problems by realising other people have much bigger mountains to climb. The conclusion being that your problem is pretty small compared to what others are having to deal with. You will be ok.

2. Ambition.

From here the rest of this book is dedicated to giving you the confidence and belief that you can get whatever you want from life. Now, here is what you also need. You need to know what you want. The problem is, most of us are pretty vague in that area starting out so let me try and help. Growing up in South Wales nobody ever told me that anything was possible. The most I could dream of was getting a good job and the life that came with that. If they did tell me, either I was not listening or the words they used just did not connect with me. So let me try my best with you.

Anything is possible! Have you got that? Shall I repeat it? Anything is possible. Seriously, anything you set your mind to over your lifetime you can achieve. Without doubt, the environment that we grow up in conditions our thinking, our expectations, our beliefs, etc. For example, if you grow up in Germany you get a German accent. Grow up in France you get a French accent. Without doubt, our environment affects how we see the world.

Here is another way of looking at it. Grow up in a place where all your friends are successful and naturally you're going to learn a thing or two about being successful. As nice as everyone was in the town I grew up in, nobody was classed as a runaway success. The issue for most of us is that less than five percent of the population is deemed as successful, so those guys are hard to find. I hope this book helps with that issue. Stripping away any limiting beliefs is the starting point to helping you achieve your full potential.

Let's start small, then scale things up. Take a look at all the stories that are out there of people who have gone from rags to riches. Find a few that inspire you. There are thousands upon thousands but ultimately all you need is just one that helps you to believe that you can achieve what you want to achieve.

 At its starting position, ambition can be relabeled as 'hope'. We all need hope. Hope that things can get better. Hope that the path ahead will get clearer and hope that life can become more enjoyable. All those things can happen but in order for the wheels to start turning you need some propulsion. That propulsion will come from what you want from life.

A great starting position is to create a list called "If anything was possible, what would you want from life?" Seriously, see what you can write. Grab a pen and a piece of paper and write away. Here are a few ideas to get you started. Pretty soon you will come up with your own.

What sort of home do you want to live in?

What sort of holidays do you want to take?

Who do you want to protect and look after?

What car do you want to drive?

Goals are critical. You will either be pushed by your circumstances or pulled by your dreams and I know which one is more fun. It's ok to write down a few selfish goals here so indulge yourself, it's your list. Write down what you want and try your best to have some fun. If this doesn't make you smile nothing will.

Go ahead, design the ultimate life. The clearer this is for you the greater your motivation will be. Once you're clear we can get started on how you are going to achieve it.

When I did this, I really decided to go for it. I created a scrap book and put pictures in there of everything I wanted to do and have. It all looked amazing and it helped me understand what I wanted for my life. It made me realise there is so much to do and so little time. If you don't have a scrap book made go ahead and do it now. It will be more fun than you can imagine and give you a clear road map of the life you want to live.

3. Vision.

Vision is a step further than ambition. Ambition is the raw material that gives meaning to your life. It's that something you can feel inside. It's often undefined in its infancy, then as you see possibilities for your life it starts to take shape and form. As you grow into adulthood it becomes a fusion of all the things you want.

You see what others have done and start to realise that you could do the same thing. Vision is you putting it all together into a clear picture that represents what you really want from life. To take the next step you now have to start defining what gives your life meaning. If you are 'wishy washy' about this you will suffer from lack of focus.

Go grab a pen and start writing about the life you want to live. If you have not made the scrapbook, put a vision board together. It's a collection of pictures that visually stimulate your mind and pull you towards the things you want to do. Take your ambition one step further and put deadlines to the trips you want to take and all the things you want to achieve with your life. Now you are getting closer.

Let me warn you though. Do it right and you are going to get pretty excited about what's ahead. One more warning: this is the last chance you will have of staying average. You know. Average job. Average car. Average holidays. Average sucks! Who wants to be Mr. or Mrs. Average? Rip up the script and go for it. Hey, this is your life, make it personal.

As much fun as all that sounds, the truth is it's not easy to detach yourself from all the things going on in your life. Even harder is detaching yourself from all the things you know that you may have messed up or feel you are not good at.

Your self-image acts as a limiting device, telling you what's not possible. You have to detach from this limiting device so I am going to share a simple technique you can use that works wonders.

Step outside your body and picture yourself in the clouds looking down on yourself. A bit whacky but hey, it works for me. It's not easy but go ahead give it a try. Go on, get up there in the clouds. Once you have practiced it a few times it will be easy. Seriously, you have to step outside your body. You can use whatever technique you want as long as it works.

Ok. Once you're up there, look down on yourself. Now you are two separate people. Perfect. It will feel weird at first but stick with me. You are now going to give yourself some words of encouragement. Try it. Imagine you are the adult who's guiding a young child. What would you say? Would you encourage the child? Would you help the child to put a vision together? Of course you would. Great, that's exactly what you need to do. If you want to make it in life you had better become your very own cheerleader and that my friend needs to start right now.

Once you have a crystal clear picture of the life you want to lead and the person you want to be, you will be surprised how strong your motivation is and how easy it will be to make decisions that advance you towards your goal.

4. Belief.

This is a big one. In fact it's huge. So many people struggle with belief in themselves. I would say it's the king pin that opens or blocks the log jam in your brain, so let's rip it apart. Without belief nothing gets off the ground. We are going to look at, what it is, where it comes from, how you keep it, what will damage it, how you repair it, how you grow it and how you transmit it to others around you.

So what is it? The initial problem is belief is not a tangible thing that you can grab hold of in the morning and slip on like a Superman tee-shirt? Or can you? Some people say you either have it or you don't. Well guess what? That's true but then again the same can be said of the Superman tee-shirt.

Let me cut to the chase. Anyone can have belief and I am going to show you how but more importantly let me tell you this first: everyone has doubts.

The reason why I am telling you this is that so many people say: "Because I have so many doubts I can't believe in myself." Let me repeat what I said. Everyone has doubts. The good news is that's where we are going to start, with you doubting yourself and struggling to believe that you can live the life that you decide to live.

Let's go to the gym for a second. Let's say you want big muscles but you have never lifted a weight before. Imagine if the personal trainer loads the bar with three hundred pounds and asks you to bench press it for ten reps. Trust me, you won't even move the bar. It takes years and years of daily discipline to get to that level of strength. It's stupid and even ridiculous to even contemplate it. Why then do people stamp their feet and scream internally: "I JUST WANT TO BELIEVE IN MYSELF!"? You can but just like the weights, you have to start small. Take baby steps and build it up.

Here is what I do. I hope you like it. I needed belief to become something tangible. Because it was invisible I just could not get my head around it, so here is what I did. As a kid I loved the Marvel comic book heroes and know that visual things work for me.

Belief became Superman, the good guy (Mr. Belief) and doubt became the bad guy (Mr. Doubt). Now when I say Superman I don't mean the cape up, up and away and all that stuff, so read on. I knew that what was going on in my head was a battle between good and bad, so why not create some characters and play the game.

So, the good guy needs some qualities and characteristics. Think of everyone who you have come across or read about that you find really inspiring, supportive and reassuring. What you're going to do here is create your own superhero. List all their best qualities until they represent all that you want to be. Once you have created your superhero (the person you want to be) he or she is going to travel with you all the way through life and protect you from all things evil. Now stay with me.

I want you to do the exact opposite in creating Mr. Doubt, the bad guy. Think about anyone and everyone that represents what you don't want to be in life. Think about all the qualities you hate and despise in others. Greed, lack of compassion, etc. The more effort you put into this the more clearly the two characters separate themselves in your mind's eye. Go on, give him a black outfit and pointy shoes like the child-catcher in Chitty Chitty Bang Bang. Frightened the life out of me!

Here is the food they like: Mr. Belief loves books, audios and people who say anything is possible, you can do it and here are the examples. Yum yum. That makes him super strong and Mr. Doubt runs away starving, crying and suffering. Perfect. Nasty bit of work he is.

Mr. Doubt loves negative people, negative news, and negative self-talk. He especially likes sentences such as "I can't do that." "I can't do this." "I am rubbish at this." "Nobody believes in me." Oh yum yum, that's what he wants.

Now, here is the great news. You and only you decide which one you are going to feed each morning when you wake up. They both sit on either shoulder at all times and they are hungry little guys, so be careful. Let the menu above act as a clear guideline to who gets what at all times.

So what is belief? Belief is an emotion. Where does it come from? Your subconscious mind. It's your good guy, Mr. Belief. How do you keep it? You feed it every day. How do you damage it? You feed its arch enemy, Mr. Doubt. How do you repair it? Take the food away from Mr. Doubt and feed Mr. Belief again. How do you grow it? You feed and nurture and pay attention to Mr. Belief every day with books, audios and association. How do you transmit it to others? You don't have to. That part is automatic. Mr. Belief has his own little transmitter and when you feed him he cranks up the transmission, simple.

5. Confidence.

Imagine if someone gave you the precise secret to developing confidence. Imagine if it was just a matter of applying a few simple formulas over time. Imagine if you woke up tomorrow morning more confident than you are today. And the next day you got better and the next day and the next day. Well, I have some great news. You can and more importantly you will be able to use these secrets instantly from today.

They have been around for thousands of years. You are not the first person in the history of mankind to want to improve their confidence. And even greater news is that super bright people have given us some easy to follow formulae. All we have to do is listen and apply their advice.

Over the last twenty-seven years I have read over a hundred books just on this subject alone. There are some truly outstanding books you can read. I will also list my favourites to help you get started but for this book I am just going to keep it simple and give you something you can apply today.

Now this is going to be your first test. We are going to find out if you are reading this book for entertainment value or whether you are reading it because you really want to start out on a better path from today.

Here is the secret. In fact it's the worst kept secret in the world and millions of people have already used it to transform their lives: "Thoughts become things." Let me repeat those words: Thoughts become things. What you hold in your mind becomes a reality in the physical world.

The pictures and visions you place in your mind stimulate your physical body to do the things that make your thoughts become a reality in the world you live.

You can rewrite that in a hundred different ways and it's worth you doing so because it will help you truly appreciate the enormity of its significance.

Marcus Aurelius, ruler of the Roman Empire wrote: "Our life is what our thoughts make it."

At some point in your life you will realise this. Control your thoughts and you will control your life.

Confident thoughts lead to confident living. It's that simple.

As we chatted about previously, this book is not about sensationalising anything. There will be no quick fix miracle messages I can offer but if you appreciate some good old-fashioned authentic advice that you're prepared to act on, I know I can help.

First of all, understand this: everyone gets nervous. Let me repeat: everyone gets nervous. You my friend are not on your own if you have ever suffered from butterflies in your stomach at the thought of just walking into a room full of strangers, then you will understand what I mean.

The fear of the unknown has terrified people for centuries. Children fear walking into a dark room. Flick the light on and in they trot. All of a sudden fear evaporates in a flash. So why is that?

Imagine if you could switch on your light and eliminate fear. Well, guess what? You can and I am going to show you how.

What changed for the child can change for you. The light allowed the child to see everything for what it really was. The light burnt away all the dark imagination that was controlling the child's emotions. The emotions controlled the physical reaction. Fear perpetuates fear and pretty soon terror sets in.

So what are confident thoughts? Where do they come from? How do you keep them? What can damage them? How do you repair them? How can you grow them and how do you project confidence to those around you?

Confidence ebbs and flows from two places: your imagined reality and your actual reality. What you believe to be happening and what is actually happening. So you have to learn to separate the two.

Let's take you back a few years. Try and think of something or some situation where you were fearful in some way or another. Dig deep. These emotions are hard to find as we store them way down in the dark recesses of our subconscious minds. For some this can be a painful procedure. For others there will be little or no drama attached. Let's take something simple and quite common. Let's say as a child you were called to the front of the room to sing a song but you forgot the words to a song.

As a child your imagined reality may be: "I forgot the words! Everyone thinks I am a fool! Nobody loves me! I am a loser! I am going to jail! My mother hates me! Where is the nearest fire exit?! Aarrrggghhh!"

The actual reality was that if the child had just walked off and said "Oops! Sorry about that. I forgot the words," everyone in the room would agree, thinking yep that's happened to me, no problem, next act.

I am sure you get the picture. As adults we have got to learn to take the drama out of the situation. The truth is though, if the child had prepared and practiced over and over it would have been a different story. So that leads us to understand practice and preparation are a major factor in boosting confidence in this is situation.

The five P's: Proper Preparation Prevents Paralysis and Poor performance. If we are prepared and we know our topic we have every reason to be confident. If we are not prepared, then we are going to need a plan B.

If you are one of the rare people who goes through life fearless, congratulations. You are in the minority. If you want to succeed in life, whatever you do, take time to study this subject. The people in your team will need you to support them, that's for sure.

We have all felt fear in varying degrees. Most of us cover it over with layers of life in the hope it will go away. It never will. Let me share a deeply personal story in the hope its lesson will help you.

My sister Dawn is one of those vibrant giving characters. If she were a firework she would be a Roman candle, full of colour life and energy.

Wednesday afternoon, 2pm, June 2002.

I released Dawn from my big arms to give her the room to breathe and speak.

Sitting in front of me she was sobbing uncontrollably. Her body trembled all over. Tears rolled down her face. She had aged ten years in a week. "Slow down babe. Take it easy. Breathe deeply. Try and relax." I said calmly. I knew I had to help her regain some control of her body.

Fear had gripped her and did not want to give up its victim without a fight. This was my sister. Fear was not going to be the winner on this day.

Slowly she started to collect herself and then she spoke. "I, I, I, I … I have got… I have got….cancer." In that moment, much like the bus accident, life slowed to a standstill. Dawn was completely and utterly consumed by fear. Her head was bowed, her nose was red, her crumpled tissue in tiny pieces from nervously twisting it over and over. She would not look at me.

I had no idea that this would be the moment but this was it. Sitting deep inside me were so many of the lessons I am trying to communicate in this book and to this day I am so grateful those lessons surfaced when I needed them most.

I was calm and I knew what I had to do.

I knew I needed to give her a massive amount of confidence.

Me: "Dawn, Dawn, look at me. You ok?"

Dawn: "No I am not ok. I have got Cancer, and of course I am not ok!"

Me: "Dawn, look at me." She raised her head. I sat there with a big reassuring smile. Deep inside me my spirit was calm and confident and already speaking to her spirit. "Well, are you going to live or die?"

Dawn : "I dont know."

Me: "Well you had better make up your mind"

Dawn: "Well I don't know OK?!"

Me: "Well you can only have one or the other, you can't have both."

Dawn: "What do you mean?"

Me: "I mean you have to choose. Are you going to live or die?"

Dawn: "Live of course."

Me: "Great. Now are you going to live a great life or a rubbish life?"

Dawn : "I dont know."

Me: "Well you are going to have to choose."

Dawn: "I am going to live a great life."

Me: "Great! Are you going to watch James grow up?" James is her son.

Dawn: "Yes."

Me: "Are you going to watch him get married?"

Dawn: "Yes."

Me: "Are you going to hold your grandchildren in your arms?"

Dawn: "Yes."

Me: "Then great! What are you crying for? Look Dawn, you get to choose what you want to believe, nobody else. Now do you like that list we just created, yes or no?"

Dawn: "Yes of course I do."

Me: "Great! For now that's all you're going to focus on. We are going to take it all one step at a time and you're going to live."

Slowly but surely we had switched the lights back on and Dawn could see a reason to fight. You have to learn to do the same.

FEAR is generally False Evidence Appearing Real. Your imagination is so powerful at creating and then exaggerating fearful images and circumstances. You have to take control and break fear down into small pieces.

When you look back on whatever it was that damaged your confidence or you were fearful of it will have two elements to it. The imagined element and the real element.

Dawn's cancer was very real and very scary but the imagination (picture) she attached to it was a hundred times scarier. I will write more on this later.

Focus on building your confidence. Make it as important as life and death because ultimately it is. All that you do with your life will be affected by the confidence with which you approach it. Confidence and fear are the flipside of the same coin. You can't choose both. It's either one or the other.

People who consistently and persistently build the muscle in their mind that gives them confidence have no problem in being confident because they have practiced it over and over until it seems they are on autopilot. It's that simple and you can do it.

6. Action.

Before you take any action, know precisely what it is that you are working towards. Make all that you do a magnificent obsession that propels you towards your specific written objectives. Having hazy goals will create hazy results.

Take time to define precisely what you want and by what date you want it. Keep your plan and goal in front of you at all times. The how to do something comes easy when we know why we are doing it.

Ultimately your actions will be the only measurement that counts. Successful people understand the difference between talking about getting something done and actually making sure the task at hand is completed.

Make your work a labour of love and you will never work a day in your life. People who truly love what they do stand out from the rest. Make a decision to be one of these people. Be the best in your field. Study anyone and everyone who has gone before you and copy their best qualities

Be decisive. Great leaders take action quickly and change their mind very slowly.

Have a sense of urgency. Life is short at best. Learn this. The quicker you get the job done the sooner you get to experience the reward that goes with it. Most painful or difficult tasks are like pulling an Elastoplast off your skin. It's better done fast.

Be quick to learn. Only a fool does the same thing over and over and expects a different result. There is an opportunity to learn in everything you do.

Question everything. What can I learn? How can I improve? How can I do better? How can I produce more in less time? As you study your actions and the actions of others, understand the impact of increasing your efficiency in the marketplace.

Say less to achieve more. Don't waffle and spend more time listening than you do talking. Put an egg timer on your desk by your phone. When you are on the phone be aware. Those grains of sand represent your life. After you have exchanged any prerequisite pleasantries, get to the point. How can I help you?

Keep a log showing what you do with every minute of every day. Do not waste a second. They all count.

Develop a little conversation map to prompt you on what to say. Stick it to your desk. Follow scripts until you're effective at dealing with all types of conversations. Study, study, study.

Life is a pantomime and people are looking for a show. I don't mean Punch and Judy, I mean you have to get as good as you can get, as fast as you can and make sure you have fun.

Be quick to forgive. You and the people around you will make mistakes. Sometimes they are going to be massive mistakes. If you spend any longer than you have to dissecting all that went wrong, you are taking time away from the positive energy you could be putting into pursuing your goals.

Study the super-achievers in your company, then copy them, then outwork them. Simple. Do that and you won't go far wrong. Don't ask others to do what you're not prepared to do. Leaders lead and that means doing the things that are uncomfortable until they become comfortable.

Learn to go the extra mile.

Developing the habit of going the extra mile will serve you well. All too often people quit when success was just around the corner. Learn to finish strong and dip over the line. Life is not a dress rehearsal, it's the real thing. Live each day like it's your last and fully appreciate the gift of life.

7. Evaluate.

This is the last and the most important section. Understanding the benefits of effective evaluation will help you make more advances than any of the other skills.

A fool repeats the same task the same way and expects a different outcome.

As you look into the details of your performance, always keep the big picture in mind. What I mean by this is always keep by your side specific written goals and objectives you are aiming to reach. This will help you keep moving in the right direction and stop you from wondering too far off track.

Make a decision right now to get better every day in every way.

Keep in mind that you are on a journey, so learn to enjoy it. Far too many people put off today's happiness in the belief that some far-off destination will hold the secret to all they wish for. When they get there and look back on life they see all the moments they could have enjoyed. Be careful this does not happen to you. Treat every day like it's your last.

Do all you can to improve all the time. Every detail counts. Here is a simple but fantastic question you should ask yourself about everything you do: "How could I have done that better?" So simple and so effective. Try it.

At ninety-nine degrees centigrade water makes a cup of tea. At a hundred degrees centigrade it creates steam and powers cities. That's only a one degree change. Sometimes in business that's all it takes, so keep searching.

Tape record yourself. Very scary at first but lots of fun. I remember listening to myself for the first time. You cannot imagine how bad I was. No wonder nobody was responding to my presentations or phone calls. I was so boring and fell into the trap of believing it was all about me and the content I was conveying. Crazy when I look back. There was no positive expectation in my voice. I asked little or no questions. I did not listen effectively. The list goes on and on.

Remember, it's all about them and what they want. Take time to get to know people.

If I had not recorded myself I would not have spotted all of these things. One by one I improved each area I was weak in. Slowly but surely I developed confidence and belief in doing the numbers and letting the right people reveal themselves.

All that time worrying and judging myself was energy wasted. Everyone gets better over time if they want to. Fail fast and learn fast is a great way to look at things. You're going to make lots of mistakes, so learn to laugh at yourself and get things done quicker.

Ask people around you who you trust and value for feedback on your presentations. How you look, how you speak and how you behave. Do not leave any stone unturned.

Be careful to pace yourself. You don't win a marathon by sprinting all the way. Find a pace you can repeat over and over consistently without getting burnt out and over time you will reach the landmarks you set.

Life is not a race, it's a race track. As long as you stay on the track you will finish the race.

It's so easy to get consumed or even overwhelmed by the details of a specific task. Always break things down into smaller elements, ensuring you never get pulled too far away from your main objective.

gauges that help to check you are making reasonable progress in reasonable time. Every project ever undertaken has used gauges to stay on track. Imagine a ship going on a long voyage. They are constantly checking gauges and reference points. Contrast the ship with a Formula 1 racing car. Again, constantly checking for the tiniest detail that can give them the edge. Remember that simple little question.

How can we do this better? One degree at a time.

Celebrate and learn to laugh at yourself.

Lastly, learn to celebrate anything and everything. Celebrate every little victory. You need to be your own best cheerleader. Life will be quick to put you down, so be sure to cheer for your team every chance you get.

Celebrate even when you mess something up. Why? Because it will teach you something and that's all you need to focus on. What can I learn from the complete train crash I just created from my actions? Honestly, learning to laugh at yourself is the most liberating thing you will ever learn. So many people are too hard on themselves. Come on, life is meant to be fun.

CHAPTER 5

QUESTIONS, MYTHS AND MISCONCEPTIONS ABOUT NETWORK MARKETING.

Questions, myths and misconceptions about Network Marketing.

In this chapter I am going to do my best to answer the main questions I am asked over and over. Before I answer them, let me make an observation straight from the coalface of dealing with people every day.

If you are looking for a reason not to get into Network Marketing you will find one.

If you are looking for a reason to get into Network Marketing you will find one.

There is no easy way for me to say it. The facts are that some people are positively and proactively searching for ways to succeed and some are searching for proof that the odds are just stacked against them and they are going to fail. Oh and it's probably someone's fault, I can hear them say.

You can read all the logic in the world on how a business can support you and your ambitions but unless there is an emotional reason why driving you, you are unlikely to take decisive action. Obviously I believe Network Marketing is a fantastic path for anyone to follow. But at the same time I understand there may be some barriers that will stop you and your emotions from trusting that statement. Let me do my best to overcome the main questions.

Is Network Marketing pyramid sales?

NO. Next question.

Just kidding. Most of the time people don't even know what they mean when they say this. Here is how a typical conversation goes:

Prospect: "Is this pyramid sales?"

Me: "Good question. I have been asked that a number of times. What is your understanding of pyramid sales?"

Prospect: "Blah blah blah…", basically explaining their understanding of what they think it is which can be a wide variation of things, culminating with: "… and the guy at the top makes all the money."

Me: "Ok, let me deal with the pyramid sales question first. I am not a specialist in pyramid sales so all I know is this." Then I draw on the following information:

Pyramid sales is a name given to a wide range of illegal recruiting scams prevalent in the '70s and '80s. People were conned into convincing friends and family into investing money into structures that promised fantastic returns on investment. Typically there were no end customer users and sometimes not even any products. The con artist ran off with the money and left thousands of people out of pocket and annoyed they had been scammed.

Because Network Marketing also encourages its distributors to introduce friends and family to the benefits of its products and opportunity, every now and then we have to explain the clear difference between the scam artists and reputable companies providing outstanding products and services to their customers through a network of distributors.

Again, let me repeat. If the prospect does not want to hear the answer you offer there is nothing you can do.

Here is a little additional assurance if you need it.

There are many multi-billion dollar turnover companies with millions of distributors all across the globe in Network Marketing. For over fifty years the industry has worked with government officials to create tight and robust legislation that protects the rights of everyone who joins Network Marketing. It's an outstanding industry, despite what the occasional minority, misinformed person chooses to think.

Life is not perfect guys. There are people for all sorts of reasons who will say black is white and white is black. It's just how it is. So if the prospect wants to believe it is an illegal pyramid scam, no problem. Let them believe it and move on.

Do the people at the top make all the money?

Model answer:

Me: "Sadly a number of people think that. Let me do my best to explain how it works in reality." Then I draw on the following information:

The precise way each Network Marketing company pays out income varies but in essence these examples will help you understand that the person who does the work gets paid the majority of the money.

Example 1: Retail income from customers.

Both distributors below operate at the retail profit margin set by the company which for this example is 50% profit.

Old established distributor makes 10 sales at £100 = £1000 turnover.

£1000 turnover x 50% profit = £500 profit.

New distributor makes 20 sales at £100 = £2000 turnover.

£2000 turnover x 50% profit = £1000 profit.

So in this example the new person makes more money because they have looked after more customers. Simple.

Example 2: Royalty income.

The company sets the royalty payment from growing and developing a team and this varies from company to company, so be sure to get the specifics from the company you are looking at. For this example let's say the company sets it at 5% royalty payment of the turnover created from the first three levels of people who join your team.

For example:

The people you introduce personally equals level 1.

The people they introduce equals level 2.

The people they introduce equals level 3.

Old established distributor never decided to do much work.

They sponsor just 2 people personally and their team copies.

Level 1 = 2

Level 2 = 4. They copy your example.

Level 3 = 8. They copy your example.

Total in your team = 14

Let's say the company's average turnover for distributors is £2000 per month.

14 x £2000 = £28,000 x 5% (the royalty commission) = £1400 per month.

New distributor is excited and wants to work.

They sponsor 10 people personally and their team copies.

Level 1 = 10

Level 2 = 100. They copy your example.

Level 3 = 1000. They copy your example.

Total in your team = 1110

Let's say the company's average turn over for distributors is £2000 per month.

1110 x £2000 = £2,220,000 x 5% (the royalty commission) = £111,000 per month.

Dramatic difference.

Please note these numbers are for illustration only as your distributors may not copy your excellent example. However it illustrates the point very clearly.

You are paid on the turnover you create, not the number of years you have been in the company. The example you set for your team and your ability to teach this example to others will dictate the size of team and turnover you build and subsequently get paid on.

Contrast that with the normal workplace where you have to try and work your way to the top over many years and you realise why people who are happy to get paid for their own personal efforts can do so well in Network Marketing.

Sounds great but my friend or relative had a bad experience.

Yes it does sound great and it is great. But it's not perfect. There are millions of people involved in Network Marketing. The chances that you or one of your friends have come across a distributor from another company somewhere along the line is pretty high. Just like anything in life, Network Marketing has its high achievers who do an amazing job at building teams and promoting outstanding customer care. Unfortunately, because of the low startup costs, it also has its fair share of people who get in and out of business with the wrong expectations and skill sets. It's these people who do the most damage to a brand.

If you or a family member have ever been approached or even pestered by an overzealous distributor trying to convince you to join their team or buy their product then please understand you are not on your own. It's also happened to me. It's not a nice experience and it damages people's perception of what we do. Worse still, you can believe that the company you are looking at will expect you to behave the same way and you could not be further from the truth.

If you allow an experience like this to stop you from finding out more about an industry that can provide you with everything you could possibly need, then that is a great tragedy. I have had terrible experiences in restaurants but it has not stopped me from dining out. I have had builders who have ripped me off but it did not stop me from building my dream home.

Do not make the mistake of defining a company or an industry based on the unprofessional behaviour of an individual or small group of people. As in any career there are good and bad examples of how to conduct yourself and I hope this book helps you to define the best path. Network Marketing has some of the most inspired and enlightened leaders you will ever find, so be careful to seek them out before forming your opinion and I assure you, the future will be very bright.

Unexpected benefits from someone who quits. Talent rolls up.

One of the remarkable things about Network Marketing is how the company's compensation plan rewards distributors who stick around for the long haul. Let me explain. When they start out most distributors are naive and lack a full set of skills. This is normal and almost the same in every line of business. It also means you may attract or even pursue the wrong type of people to join your team. The net result of this means you can occasionally introduce someone who is high maintenance and produces very little. This can be frustrating and give you the wrong image of what your future business will look like once it has matured. During these periods and without a full understanding of what can happen long term, some distributors decide to quit, believing the people they have introduced will never amount to anything. What they failed to realise is people can and do change over time.

So let's say someone you introduce brings in three people who really don't look like they will amount to much. The person you introduced for one reason or another leaves the company and moves on to something else. Again, this is natural. People often try a number of things before they find what they love to do. The three people he or she introduced however fell in love with their journey, committed to their personal development and over time go on to build huge businesses. They all roll up as if they had been personally introduced by you. So even though you originally sponsored one person who was not that great, you end up with three fantastic team builders.

You never know who your team are going to bring in, so stick around.

I am not a salesperson so can I do this?

Yes you can, but again only if you really want to. Let me try and reassure you.

The facts are that the vast majority of people who succeed in Network Marketing are not aggressive salesman personality types. The salesman personality generally wants to make a fast buck and has very little patience. Any serious business takes time.

People often use the line "I am not a salesperson" to get them off the hook of having to step outside their comfort zone and learn new skills.

The real truth is, it's got nothing to do with whether or not you are a salesperson, it's got everything to do with how you manage your inner fears and insecurities.

Rewritten, the inner thoughts behind the statement "I am not a salesperson" could look like this:

"I'd love to do this but I lack the confidence. My self-image will not allow me to believe I can learn, improve and perform in a changing environment. So I am going to use the classic line 'I am not a salesperson' in the hope that the person opposite me buys my excuse."

Don't let your fear of failure hold you back.

Let's cut to the chase. The vast majority of people are not born salespeople. Network Marketing companies thrive and survive because they appeal to the masses not the minority. They provide outstanding ongoing training on how to succeed and develop as a person and the best bit is that everyone else in the company is on the same path as you. Imagine a whole new group of friends with the same ambition. Not only does it sound great, in reality it's amazing and I can't wait for you to experience it.

People who feel they are not salespeople at the beginning often become the highest achievers. Why? Because when you make a decision to face your fears and grow as a person you show others the way. They see where you have come from and this makes you relatable and approachable, as opposed to the super-slick individuals who everyone looks at and says: "Well there is no way I can be like them."

I have no time to start a business.

There are twenty-four hours in any given day. How you invest your time will determine the life you live.

If you have no time right now, that's the very reason you should consider changing how you use your time. Earlier I wrote that successful people invest their time into creating assets that generate money.

If I could show you how to invest ten hours into a business and get a hundred back in return would that be a good investment? Let's put it another way. If you put ten pounds in the bank and after thirty days the ten pounds became a hundred pounds, would that be a good return?

Obviously the answer is yes. Let's look again at how a Network Marketing business can help you leverage your time.

Let's say you switch off the TV, make a few changes to your diary and create maybe ten hours per week that you are going to dedicate to building a better life. Fifty percent of this time you dedicate to looking after your own retail customers. Fifty percent of the time you use to present your new business to people.

Ten people join your team and each decides to invest ten hours the same as you. Now your business will have a total of a hundred and ten hours per week being invested into its growth.

Look at that simple explanation again. Imagine a business that can grow at ten times the time investment that you are personally investing into it.

You put in ten hours, your team (and remember there are only ten of them) put in ten hours each and that gives you a return of a hundred hours! Imagine having a hundred people in your team. Your business will then have a thousand hours per week being invested into its expansion. That's the power of return on investment you can create in Network Marketing. My suggestion to you is make the time to invest and change your relationship with how you invest your time.

My partner won't let me do it.

Believe it or not this is actually quite a popular statement. As incredulous as it seems, some people allow other people to totally control their lives twenty-four-seven.

Let's deal with the partner first.

Many times a partner will give the other partner an ultimatum as to whether they are allowed to start their own business. Let's analyse this. If you brought home an extra five thousand pounds cash and said: "Here you go. I just made this money from my new business and wanted to give it to you", would they be upset?

Of course not. So the bottom line is it's a belief, trust, or confidence issue.

All of which can be overcome with education, patience, evidence and results.

You have to treat the partner's concerns with compassion and patience. At all times, the last thing you want to do is create any animosity.

It's common for one out of two people to be excited, so just be sensitive to the fact that confidence grows as they see results.

If the partner stops the other person in their tracks and refuses to allow them to get started then there is nothing you can do. You are looking for people who are at least strong enough to stand up for their own rights. If they are not prepared to do this it is highly unlikely they will succeed in business.

Just be thankful that you have your own freedom of thought and move on.

My boss won't let me do it.

This is a sensitive one so let's be even more careful. Some companies will tell their employees that they cannot do this, that or the other with their free time away from work. Obviously there are justifiable reasons why certain employers will have an active interest in making sure there is no conflict of interest in what their staff do in their spare time. But there are limits to their power.

Employers have to be careful not to expect to be able to exert an unreasonable amount of control over someone's life. My advice is to be professional and honest at all times. I have many police officers in my team who have to follow a clear procedure for declaring their intended activities even before they sign up. I can assure you it only acts to increase their enthusiasm to start when they have to wait for clearance and does not slow them down in any way.

In other sectors you need to be sure to explain to your employers that you fully respect the professional boundaries of your job. But at the same time you want to be clear that you are starting a business part-time from home outside of any company commitments. Work with the employer to help them understand that your new venture will have nothing but a positive impact on your performance and you should be fine.

Will your job status prevent you from becoming more?

So often I come across really nice people who would do extremely well in Network Marketing but they are trapped by the status, confidence or familiarity their job or career position offers them. Again, let me be very clear. I am not trying to dishonour any job or career. I just see so many people progress and then over time they stop having fun. They get stuck and work becomes a little mundane. Nobody consciously makes a commitment to stop growing as a person. Life just seems to stall at a certain point. Your career gets stale and loses its sparkle. You look around at all your options and consider trying something new. The next few paragraphs may change your destiny, so read it carefully.

Breaking free will require a huge amount of courage. You are very competent within your field of expertise and any new venture will be a journey into the unknown. But if you have an itch, you had better scratch it. If there is one thing I know for certain, when you look back on your life as this book is forcing me to do, you will remember all the things you should have done but for one reason or another you simply did not do. If you retreat from something that you feel you should do it will nag away at you all your life.

Try and see beyond where you are at the moment. As I stated above you may be in a superb job and life is great. Honestly I could not be happier for you but be careful. Things change and when they do, if you're not prepared it can hit you hard. Don't let your status stop you from learning new skills.

Your job title should not define you. Your vision of who you are should define you. Don't become the "job". Do the "job" you are paid to do as well as you can. At the same time have a clear vision of the life you want to live. It's easy to fall into the trap of living the life your position allows you to live. There is a brave new world out there so have courage and be true to yourself at all costs.

You can make excuses or you can make money but you can't make both!

That about sums it up. I have done my best to offer sensible solutions to the main questions that crop up. But if you don't have the ambition to press ahead, there is nothing I can say that will help you overcome your perceived barriers to starting.

CHAPTER 6

WHAT CAN YOU GAIN FROM A NETWORK MARKETING CAREER?

What can you gain from a Network Marketing career?

Let's talk about freedom of choice for a moment and why I think Network Marketing is a better option than a career in the long run. Outside of my Network Marketing world of friends I mix with an incredibly wide range of people from all walks of life and I am very grateful for that.

A number of them have successful careers and a number of them are just about getting by. Either way they are a great bunch of fun-loving people, just a normal society mix.

Here is what I have noticed. Very few of them have the sort of time and money freedom that is commonplace in a Network Marketing career. That's not a criticism in any way, it's just an observation. Most jobs require very structured and disciplined hours of attendance. If that's what people want then no problem, it's just that I like to play golf and when the sun shines midweek I wish I had a few more mates to play with, that's all. If your goal is creating more freedom of time, the great news is that's one of the principle ambitions in Network Marketing.

I would even hazard a guess that few people ever ask themselves the simple question: "How can I create time and money freedom to allow myself to do all the things I want to do?"

Most people do what the next person does, which is get the best job they can and just accept what comes with the territory. I want you to question that.

The vast majority of people jump on the fast lane of a career and never even notice the exit signs marked "Here is the life you want but you're just not looking"

All I am trying to do is get you to look at a few country roads. So many people are busy being busy they don't even realise there are other paths in life that may be more attractive. Life rushes by and before you know it you have climbed the ladder of success but it's leaning against the wrong wall.

Giving a hundred percent of your time to your employer I personally feel is insanity. No career pays well enough to demand a hundred percent of your every waking minute. Great to give them the very best of fifty percent of your life but be sure to invest the other fifty percent in creating all the other elements that you want in your life.

There have been many great philosophers over time and one thing's crystal clear from what I have read. Balance in all things is very important. Fifty percent is enough.

Running your own business gives you great real life experience. There's nothing better than having ownership of something that reflects who you are and becomes your creation. For improving your skills and understanding of what life has to offer there is no parallel.

Built correctly here is what a Network Marketing business looks like.

You start part-time in your spare hours alongside your job or career. Over a number of years you steadily build up your business giving you additional income and the freedom to choose which career path appeals to you most. Your life skills grow and develop which also reflects positively on your career path.

The parent company you have chosen to join produces outstanding products and or services. Distributors within the company have the opportunity to create two clear forms of income as previously illustrated, income streams 1 and 2.

You personally develop strong customer acquisition and support skills. You teach this to the people you introduce and ensure they teach the people they introduce, helping you develop your leadership skills.

The whole organisation is supported by excellent online and offline training. As you grow you place extra focus on developing your leadership skills to be the very best they can be. You identify and develop from within your team strong leaders, capable of running their business with or without you and encourage them to follow your lead.

At some point in your career, as your leadership emerges and matures, you become largely redundant in the day-to-day results of your business. Your role then evolves into more of a leadership mentoring role as you guide your key leaders to greater personal success.

Do this effectively over many years, focusing on outstanding customer service and the vast majority of your income will justifiably be royalty based, i.e. it comes in whether you work or not.

That's called financial freedom.

The life skills you will develop as a business owner.

It's almost impossible to underestimate the wide range of life skills that you pick up in the process of actually building a Network Marketing business. It offers astonishing value when compared with what you would have to pay in other fields to get exposed to the same level of education and teaching.

Network Marketing companies put a strong focus on offering comprehensive life skills training to their distributors because they want them to succeed in a competitive world. Over the years the industry has seen what well trained distributors can achieve. Other industries are rarely as sharp in these areas so for this alone it's a great career choice.

Doing an MBA is a great start but actually being out there at the coalface is where you really get to know what you are made of.

Communication skills:

Watching and listening to dynamic leaders explain in great detail every single step of their journey allows you to listen, learn, duplicate and then refine how you deliver what you have heard. It's the ultimate mentoring culture.

Leadership skills:

Network Marketing's prime commodity is people. All the great leaders in the industry who new distributors learn from have acquired and developed superb leadership skills. Each leader will have studied and then applied their knowledge in the field. Rarely will you ever be in an environment where every single leader started at the bottom and worked their way to the top. In Network Marketing there is no old boys group that opens the door for a special chosen few. In this industry you are paid on performance. It's as simple as that.

Organisation skills:

To grow, develop and manage the expectations of a team of distributors from diverse backgrounds and skill sets will test your organisation skills to the max. You will need time management, financial competence, delegation, and key performance indicator (KPI) skills to name only a few.

Entrepreneurial skills:

If you have never been in a room with a group of passionate entrepreneurs you had better prepare yourself. I have lost count of the amount of times that battle-hardened people have been blown away as they walked into a training room where two hundred to twenty thousand distributors are ready for a top-class training.

The energy, anticipation and excitement in the room are electric. You instinctively feel at home and don't want to leave. Being around like-minded people who want the most from life lifts your confidence and belief to new levels and you start to shake off some of the rust that being in the wrong space may have given you.

Big picture thinkers.

Developing a vision for the possibilities that are ahead of you in life is often something that only comes with experience. It's a chicken and egg scenario. I promise you this: ask anyone over fifty if they would like to have known when they were twenty what they know now and here is what you will see. Their face will light up, followed by a large sigh. Then you will get the "If I knew then what I know now" speech. Then, slowly but surely you will see a hint of sadness appear. In that moment, I assure you, they are thinking they could have used the time more wisely.

In Network Marketing you get a chance to learn from people who have travelled the path you are about to travel. You would be crazy not to listen attentively.

Positive Association.

Yet another benefit of being in a Network Marketing culture is the melting pot of ambition and personal development that's commonplace in every company.

Being mindful of who you spend the majority of your time with is critical. Developing a close-knit group of ambitious, bright, hard-working friends will serve to keep you on track. By contrast, having the wrong group of friends will pull you away from all the daily disciplines that will advance you towards your goals.

While on the subject of friends, one of the most enjoyable and unexpected aspects of developing a Network Marketing career is the friendships you will form. It's interesting; so many distributors comment that they value these friendships higher than any material reward. As we grow as adults we learn to be more discerning about whom we want to be around. Having a huge pool of people to choose from with common goals is a refreshing change to difficult, uninspiring conversations that can happen if your world has become too small.

Financial security.

Short-term (0-2 years):

Most people join initially to see if they can make an extra £500 to £2000 and there is nothing wrong with that. Typically people are looking to use their Network Marketing career to pay off student debt, save for a holiday, help with the mortgage or get a new car. These are not huge lifestyle ambitions. They are more related to survival and quality of life. Many job incomes have a ceiling that you can't get past. Having your own business just gives some more flexibility.

Mid-term (2-5 years):

This is where it starts to get very exciting. When you first join you are hoping it will work. Scared, uncertain but enthusiastic you take the plunge. After a year or two you have learned all the basic skills of developing an income and you understand the culture of the company and what you need to do to climb higher.

At this point you will start to realise it's only you, your self-image and your skill set that dictates how much you will earn. You will meet literally thousands of people who have done what you want to do, so why not you? That's why Network Marketing companies encourage such a strong personal develop-ment culture. They understand your business will grow in proportion with your growth as a person.

For those with a greater ambition, Network Marketing can offer some of the highest paid careers in the world.

Long-term (5 years plus):

This is when the real value of Network Marketing comes through. All the work you did on yourself in the early years starts to benefit you. Long gone are your initial insecurities. You are now on a clear path to becoming a relaxed, skills-driven distributor who knows your numbers, executes your plans and is happy to be fully accountable for your results. Welcome to the world of being a Network Marketing Professional.

Residual income and time freedom.

Many people develop a Network Marketing business simply because they want more time freedom and flexibility. They have decided to turn their backs on an alarm clock and commute existence in exchange for working from home.

Quality of life can easily be scarified if you allow yourself to be consumed by the increasing hours and demands of a modern career; sadly this is becoming all too common. Instead of spending lazy summer evenings taking a stroll by the ocean or in the country, some people are trapped in a commuting prison. It does not have to be that way. But it will only change if you take deliberate and decisive action to create the life you want.

The recipe that represents success is different for everyone but most would include having enough time and enough money to do what they want to do. In Network Marketing, once you have built a large organisation, the income continues to come in whether you are working or not as you are paid on turnover. Whether you are on the beach or in the office it does not matter, that's your choice and trust me it's a fantastic feeling. Much like the royalties you receive from the initial effort put into writing a book, your efforts go into creating your business asset that continues to produce and pay you long after you stop working.

The tax advantages of being self-employed.

There are many great tax advantages to being self-employed. Obviously it's vital to stick carefully to the rules and guidelines as set out by the tax authorities, so seek professional advice from an accountant as early as possible to ensure you keep clear records that keep you on the safe side of the law. Please do not underestimate the importance of being organised and on track with your general administration. There is nothing worse than being disorganised and there is nothing better than being on track and feeling secure.

For now, here is just a short list to make you aware that being self-employed may be a good option for you alongside a career. As you review the list please be clear, you can only claim expenses that directly relate to you running your own business. So let's look at the list of things you can claim tax relief for.

Communications: phone, mobile phone, Internet, costs of calls and equipment.

Travel expenses: train, bus, airfare, taxis hotel and meals for overnight stays.

Car: car petrol or diesel, running costs like tyres, garage bills for car repair, hire charges, breakdown recovery polices etc.

Office expenses: computers, laptops, software, office equipment, education tools, books audios, stationary, postage.

Rent rates and leasing: office space rent and rates, a percentage of areas used at home for business, leased equipment.

Professional services: accountancy, legal services, insurance, training courses, etc.

Financial charges: bank charges, professional fees, insurance indemnities, interest on HP polices, etc.

General business: advertising across all mediums, website charges, mail, product samples, insurance, certain clothing, cost of any goods or services purchased for business, building and construction specific to business.

As you can see, running a business alongside your chosen career can open the door to you having far more choice in how you present yourself for taxation and is something I strongly recommend if you want to control your own financial destiny.

Parties and holidays.

There is a strong culture of reward and celebration in all Network Marketing companies. They appreciate everyone is self-employed and as such distributors look forward with great anticipation to attending the lavish parties and glamorous vacations they can qualify for. We have been fortunate enough to be invited to some of the most amazing locations in the world and would never in a million years have been able to experience this in a conventional career.

No significant financial risk.

Getting started in any business costs money and in most cases a significant amount of money. One of the great things about Network Marketing is most companies allow you to get started for less than two hundred pounds. From day one you can focus on creating a retail income and quickly get your business into positive cash flow. That's almost unheard of in conventional business but very common in Network Marketing.

Wide selection of companies.

There is a wide selection of companies with an even wider selection of products and services to choose from. Choose the one that appeals to you most. Study Chapter 8 on "How to choose the right company" and you will be on your way to an exciting new future. Great Network Marketing companies and their leaders encourage strong respectful bonds between all lines of distributors to protect the brand and the industry to ensure we all rise as one team.

Being part of the Network Marketing world.

Network Marketing has to be one of the best kept business secrets in the world. How else can you start a business with limitless benefits for next to nothing? I have spent the major part of my life reading and studying about business and the various routes to market and I have found nothing that even comes close.

It's the most dynamic and exciting sector in any industry and I encourage you to find out more with passion and confidence.

Today I travel all over the world helping people exit frustrating careers and apply their drive and determination into their own business. It's fantastic to watch them come alive right before my eyes and then over time grow into the vision they create for themselves and their family.

If you are keen to get started or just find out more about the various companies you can work with, I will make sure you have a pathway into whatever field you choose.

CHAPTER 7

WHAT ARE THE MAIN REASONS PEOPLE FAIL OR SUCCEED IN NETWORK MARKETING?

What are the main reasons people fail or succeed in Network Marketing?

There are many different reasons why people fail or succeed at various things in life and hopefully through the course of this book we will cover them all. Network Marketing is no different. The key to this chapter is helping you identify the things that will hold you back, then show you what you will need to drive you forward.

Once you know what these differences are then it's simply a matter of aligning yourself with the things that help you succeed as opposed to those that lead to failure. It's not rocket science or smoke and mirrors. It's laid out plain and simple for you below. As you study the list below, please remember this: it's ok to have weaknesses, as long as you recognise them and begin the process of turning the weakness into a strength. Here is the first one:

Poor versus positive mental attitude.

If you project poor or weak belief in your product or service, your prospect will gain no confidence in getting a result with what you have to offer and the truth is it's all about them and their confidence. People buy people. If you don't have a positive mental attitude at the start it's vital to develop one as quickly as you can. Remember it's about the service you offer and not about you as a person, so relax and focus your words on the benefits to the consumer.

Everyone has a few skeletons in the cupboard. Times when you messed up. No problem. Forgive yourself for any past failings and make a decision that your new company represents an exciting new future for you. The vast majority of people who you will come across are people looking for clear direction. They want to make a decision that will move them forward towards a better future, so just focus on offering them some simple steps they can take and you will be surprised at how well you do.

A classic example of putting pressure on yourself is creating the belief that you need to have all the answers and be great at everything in order for people to connect with what you are offering and this is simply not true. The prospect wants to gain access to one of three things. The product you offer, the service you offer or the business opportunity you offer. It's not about you! With that in mind, the faster you get out of the way the better. Take yourself out of the equation and put all focus on what you offer. When you adopt this approach it not only takes the pressure off you, it also takes the pressure off everyone in your team as they adopt the same position.

Now everyone has the opportunity to develop a positive mental attitude because it's about having belief in what you offer and that's something everyone can have in an instant.

Lazy versus serious student

Far too often I see new people who are complacent with learning the basic fundamentals that will drive their new business forward. It's understandable that some people will get caught in the headlights initially. Going into business for yourself is an exciting opportunity but being lazy simply does not cut it.

Being excited is great but as quickly as possible you must move from the romantic "Waw this looks exciting!" phase, into the "I am deadly serious about my business!" phase. All you do then is study and focus on the skills that will drive you forward. In most companies there are only five or six things you need to learn to do really well. My advice is find out what they are as fast as you can by asking lots of questions at every opportunity.

Make a decision to be a serious student and you will be on track for whatever level of success you aim for. Sit on the front row of every single meeting you are allowed to attend. Be the first to arrive and the last to leave, tape record everything and once more ask lots and lots of questions.

An ego driven by arrogance that stops you from learning versus an ego guided by humility and a passion to learn from those around you.

It's essential to have an ego but it's also critical to use it in the correct way. There are few things more damaging than a big ego that stops you from listening effectively to others who are trying to help you. Too many people waste time by trying to develop their new business using bad habits they picked up before coming into Network Marketing.

I am not saying it's impossible to bring great skills to the table from day one. For sure that will be an asset but be careful. Stay humble, park your opinion and learn from people who have already done what you want to do before your ego gets in the way of you moving ahead. You were born with two ears and one mouth. Be sure to use them in that proportion. By committing to the learning process and being a great student you also set a great example for your team to follow and trust me, people do what you do, not what you tell them to do.

Bad time management versus excellent time management

Bad time management is one of those silent assassins present in the death of every business. It just eats away at the foundations until the whole structure comes tumbling down. Taking too long to complete the simplest of tasks robs you of any free time you were hoping to create. Lawyers keep a record of every minute used in their day because they value their time plus they know what to charge. You should be equally as focused on monitoring your time usage.

There is nothing worse than a waffling distributor who fails to get to the point. Successful people say less to achieve more. Successful people are always asking the question "How can I be more efficient with my time?"

Give a teenager all day to clean their room with no specific reward and it still doesn't get done. Give them twenty minutes in exchange for two tickets to their ultimate rock concert and they will have it done with ten minutes to spare. There are many ways to increase production using a host of rewards that do not need to revolve around money. Just think out of the box. Study time management books and make a decision to be as efficient as possible.

A sure way to fail is not deciding what your priorities are in advance of any use of your time. Decide upfront before completing any task what your reasons are for doing it and what you will get if you do a great job. Focus on the reward and the task is easy!

Get organised. Henry Ford conducted time and motion studies in his factories. Simple things like having nuts and bolts at hand, as opposed to walking to fetch them, saved thousands of man-hours. Where can you save seconds, minutes, hours? It all counts. Always ask yourself how you can be more efficient.

Ineffective communication versus effective communication.

Your success will be hugely impacted by how you communicate. Remember the marketplace will only ever respond to what you say or do and how you look. The reaction you get from the market will always depend on the effectiveness of your communication. And remember it's always about them and what they want and not about you and what you want.

Listen observe and think deeply before you speak or act. Know your audience. Gather enough facts. Look to understand their position completely. Be a great listener.

All too often we give our view and opinion before gathering the information that would allow us to make the connection we are looking for. I often get too excited and make this mistake, then kick myself for acting too impulsively.

Take a moment to ask yourself what they want, what they're after and how you can help them. Once you understand these things then you can consider what they need to hear.

How can you present your point in a fashion that helps them to have the belief and confidence in your offering that allows them to take positive action? What words, images and actions will help them feel you are the person who can help them?

Complicated presentations that nobody understands versus simple, clear and fun presentations that people totally understand.

All too often I see enthusiastic distributors 'vomit' far too much information all over people. They feel they can dazzle them with the amazing facts and figures about their company, product or service and then expect the prospect to jump out of their chair and say "I am in!" This is a classic example of the distributor saying and feeling "listen to me" as opposed to the distributor thinking about how they can listen to them first.

Let me give you a better path. Whether it's a one to one or group presentation always look to disarm anyone in front of you. It's hard to be negative to someone who smiles and is genuinely nice. Be humble and empathetic at the start. Use soft, gentle, engaging and friendly words. Don't scare people away before you have even started. The aim is to connect with your audience.

Use simple phrases like "I knew nothing at the beginning. I had little confidence. In fact I was terrible and never thought I could do this. But once I gathered a few facts I felt comfortable that this opportunity would suit anyone who wants to get ahead, so I hope that connects with you." This is reassuring to the new person who more often than not is asking themselves, "I wonder if I can do this"

First keep it simple. Second keep it fun.

People want and need things to be simple and having fun is always a bonus in a world that can get a little too serious.

Here is what I mean by simple: strip away any detail that is just not needed.

Make a decision to enjoy what you do. It's infectious and people like being around people who are having fun and enjoying themselves. If it seems like hard work to you it will seem like hard work to them.

Decide in advance what the primary benefits are that you offer and focus on these. Study all the details on your products and services with the ambition to be able to speak about them in easy to understand layman's terms. Communicate in simple bite-sized pieces and frequently ask "Is that clear?" You're looking to create the thought in their mind that anyone can do what you do.

If you go charging ahead trying to be impressive and lose them halfway you will never get them back. They will pretend they are not interested when the truth is you went too fast, they did not like you as a person and they did not understand. No matter what the question just navigate back to the basics of what you offer. Be patient, smile lots, look like you enjoy what you do and make it easy for them to see a benefit for themselves.

If you ever get stuck or you're asked an awkward question, just be honest. Use phrases like "I have only recently got started and whilst I am excited, truthfully I don't know the answer to that. But what I do know is this…" Then just reiterate the benefit of what you offer. If they are adamant they need to know something specific, lean on your company support materials. Pretty much everything they need to know will be printed on your company literature so just focus on building a relationship and guiding them to where they can find the info they need. Just be likeable. This just makes you human and far more attractive than someone trying to give them the unattractive big sell. If they don't find what they are looking for, no problem. You tried to help but you can't. Just move on. The onus is on them, not you. It's their life.

The more you know and understand, the more comfortable you will become. But this takes time so you need a get-out clause. In the beginning use this: "Don't ask me too many questions, I am new." This line works great, especially with powerful compassionate people, the very candidates you look for. They look at you and think gosh, if that person can do it I am going to get rich. BOOM!

No team spirit versus outstanding team spirit.

This is one of my favourite topics as I grew up in a team culture. In many ways rugby was my family, my school and my church in my formative years.

A team of average players who will live or die for each other will always beat a team of superstars focused on their own personal agenda. There is nothing on earth like being part of an amazing team. It floods your body with belief, confidence, camaraderie and passion to be the servant that allows the team to cross the line.

Take a look at some of the recent interviews with team-based sports men and women who have achieved astonishing success and the first words that come from their mouths will be "I would not be here without the team."

These are the cream of the crop. The kings and queens of sporting endeavour and what do they focus on? Team. It's all about team spirit.

By contrast, look at the celebrity obsessed culture that prevails in the media. Everyone having to watch their backs. Every little detail scrutinised and no room for imperfection or mistakes.

Ask yourself which culture you would prefer to be a part of. To be surrounded by people that have toiled by your side, people who have cried, laughed and bled with you where everyone appreciates each other's talents and nobody feels the need to own the spotlight. Or to be the one success story that is singled out on their own as the perfect human being that never makes mistakes. Personally, I would not want that pressure.

Network Marketing is all about teamwork and developing team spirit.

A chain is only as strong as its weakest link. I am so grateful that in my early years we were all taught to operate as a team. To protect and support any weak spots in our team no matter what. It was all for one and one for all. There was no room for superstars or celebrities. It still sounds heroic today. Even now as I read this it makes me smile. I still love it. Where is my rugby ball?

Problem oriented versus being solution oriented.

It's vital you move away from the masses of people who are problem oriented and navigate across to becoming the solution oriented leader you know you can be.

The dynamic leaders within our team are fantastic people to be around. They are presented with the same tangled path through life that we all have to face but instinctively they know they have to find a way forward.

Time after time the distributors who require the least amount of attention and input out-produce the distributors clamouring for extra attention. At the end of the day it's about making things happen and that responsibility lands squarely on the individual who wants to enjoy the rewards.

Here is just one of the many lines I heard my dad bark out to the electricians under his command while working in the heat of the steelworks. It's late into the night, everyone is under pressure trying to get the steelworks rolling again and many of the guys are telling my dad what can't be done. Here was his response to one such moment:

"Ron, I don't want to hear how it can't be done. I know lots of ways it can't be done. Find a way to get it working. Work it out and then get back to me. We are not going home until that happens."

When it boils down to it most issues drop into the plain and simple file. You either get the job done or you don't. And the truth is, when your back is firmly against the wall your sense of urgency kicks in and your performance shifts dramatically.

I see far too many distributors who are so caught up in the problem that they can't see the solution. As I mentioned earlier in the book, great leaders have the ability to step outside or above the problem and look at the bigger picture. Practice this until it's second nature.

Let's start this process right now. Picture one of the problems you currently believe you have or maybe caught up in. Now picture as clearly as you can the consequences of it really going bad. In other words the worst case scenario. And trust me, yes I really mean the worst case scenario. Now you know how bad it can be. Take a moment to contemplate that outcome. Once you feel the pain and discomfort of knowing what you don't want you can begin to picture the opposite that represents what you do want.

Now step outside your body or remove yourself from the problem and begin to brainstorm the pathway to creating what you truly want. Think of actions, thoughts and beliefs which are opposite to the ones you were previously consumed by. Shift your thinking and your direction a hundred and eighty degrees away from the outcome you know you do not want to experience and you will be heading towards what you do want. Become obsessed with being a solution oriented person. Don't wish for nothing to test you. Life will always test you. Accept this as part of the game and make a decision to become more. Welcome challenges no matter how complex and difficult they seem to be. See them for what they truly are, an opportunity for you to display your skill set in finding solutions and show the world what you are capable of.

Making excuses versus doing whatever it takes.

We all know people who have turned making excuses into a fine art. Instead of taking full responsibility for the results that come from their actions they look to blame anyone they can to offload any responsibility. Rather than accept that it will only ever be down to them to change what the marketplace gives back to them, they invent mythical influences that conspire to pull down any ambition they have. Whilst you and I know this is complete nonsense, it's often hard to get people to accept these simple laws.

Sadly, something else they fail to realise is that when they point the finger of blame away from their own actions they relinquish all power to change whatever outcome they seek to influence.

My advice is make a decision here and now to never allow yourself to give away your power to change an outcome by putting blame at someone else's feet. You can make excuses all day long but one thing you can't do is make excuses and progress at the same time. If you ever catch yourself making the classic "It's not my fault, I am a victim" speech, stop! Take stock and reread the above.

Create a new brand for yourself. Become known as the person who 'does whatever it takes' all the time to 'get the job done'. People gravitate to people they know are winners as opposed to whiners. It's critical to set yourself apart from the crowd. By building your reputation as someone who does whatever it takes you become the person others look up to and take direction from. You cannot demand respect, it's something you earn through your actions.

Using your words to put yourself down as opposed to talking yourself up.

Every now and then you will hear people say "I am rubbish at this, that or the other." This is one of those instinctive things we do as we run around on auto pilot trying to get everything done. Careful, over time if you don't learn to manage these little conversations effectively they can lead you to catastrophic results. How you manage your inner voice and subsequently how you speak to yourself have huge consequences. Sadly, few people are even aware of how your subconscious can and will be programmed by the voice in your head.

Most people carry on blissfully ignorant of how they are sabotaging their own performance. People who want to become successful simply do not have the luxury of negative self-talk. Putting yourself down or even allowing yourself to utter doubt about your expectations, self-image or performance in any way will only compound any fearful beliefs you may have. Do you honestly think the number one golfer in the world Rory McIlroy stands over a putt saying to himself "Maybe I am going to miss this shot."? No way. I can assure you, on every shot he will be visualising over and over the perfect outcome and on top of that he will have his inner voice under control, repeating over and over "This is easy, I can do this. That ball is dropping in the hole."

Without doubt you have to become your own best cheerleader. You have to talk yourself up at every single opportunity. I don't mean shouting out silly meaningless phrases into the air. I am talking about something deeply personal. Something that really means something to you. Take time to think about this subject. It will be a part of everything you become in life. How you counsel yourself has a huge bearing on your performance.

Sit down and write inspiring letters and notes to yourself. Tell yourself how wonderful you are. Set goals. Remind yourself that you are solution oriented and fill your letters with all the aspirational qualities that you wish to represent. As I type, it stirs strong emotions from deep inside me. Clearly some of the cuts and scrapes from my past are not fully healed. Although today I live a very privileged life, I could never dream of forgetting where I came from. It wasn't easy to break free from some of the chains I inherited in a working class environment. As stated earlier, there are many things I am extremely grateful for but some things just had to go if I was to move on. The same will be the case for you. Allowing the wrong thoughts to dominate your mind will not serve you well. My mind was like a fertile untended garden. Lots going on but totally out of control. I needed to focus and you will too.

When I first read advice like this I thought waw, that's a little deep and I am not sure if I can change in the ways I need to. What will my friends think? Isn't this a little silly or over the top? Well guess what? Here is a newsflash: for things to change, you must change. It's as simple as that.

Certain friends did decide to poke fun and remind me to get back in line. Certain friends said things like "Who do you think you are?" as if ambition was a disease. Then certain friends just smiled and said "Crack on son, you can do it." Guess which ones are still friends today.

Life will be quick to put you down and you will need plenty of internal resolve to rebuff the naysayers you will come across. It's rare to start out on a new career in a business that few people understand and then have people queuing up to congratulate you and offer to support you on your journey. I really wish it was different but it's not, it just does not work that way. You are going to have to fight.

Network Marketing is full of visionary people who are up for the fight. It's still new in many people's eyes and as a result you will have to work hard to explain your choice. That's one of the reasons I wrote this book, to help you communicate the truth about our industry in a fashion that is authentic and acceptable by the masses.

Make a decision to join us and you will be surrounded by new friends who will represent everything I write about. It's amazing and I love it.

Get it all right and the outcome equals great momentum and you charge ahead.

When you get it right and momentum comes your way it's a wonderful experience.

The truth is though, it's very rare to create serious momentum from day one. It's something you build towards over time. Of course there are a select few people who arrive with an extremely well-polished skill set. When this happens and if they are able to weave their skills into the business plan of the company they choose to join, exciting things can happen.

For the vast majority of people who join Network Marketing, the acquisition and refinement of these skills takes a minimum of two to five years, so you are going to need patience with yourself and your team.

Over time, all that we have discussed can and will come together if you have a burning ambition to make it that way. As you grow and learn, so do those around you and at some point on your journey a perfect storm of opportunity and preparation will arrive. When this happens be ready and willing to take advantage of the opportunity that presents itself. Hopefully you will have refined and practiced all your skills and your work ethic will be fueled by confidence and belief in your ability to rise to the top.

Your future is only limited by your ambition and belief in what's possible for you so make one more decision to be the best you can and let the games begin.

CHAPTER 8

CHOOSING THE RIGHT COMPANY. THE TOP TEN FACTORS YOU NEED TO CONSIDER.

Choosing the right company. The top ten factors you need to consider.

Before you choose which company you are going to get started with look carefully at the information below. There are many different companies with a wide range of products, services and operating methods.

Choose one that really resonates with you. Something that you want to be a part of. Something that you will represent with pride in the marketplace. Do this and you will be making a big step forward with your chances of success.

Let me give you an example. I work in the field of helping people to achieve personal transformations. Our ambition is to help people to get into the best shape of their life through a combination of improved diet choices, regular exercise and achievable lifestyle changes. I love watching the confidence of our customers grow as they gain control of their lives and look for people who are attracted to a similar career. Find a company that helps you feel the same emotions and you will be on your way to success.

Although you can start your Network Marketing business at any age, look for cultures that promote and progress youth into the business. Feeding young people into your company means the business will have more longevity. It takes time for people to develop all the qualities required for success in any business. Whatever company you choose, if they are not focused on reaching out to and providing dedicated support to young people you will be missing a trick. Middle-aged and older distributors can bring outstanding skill sets and as such are also essential to stable growth but be careful to mix up the blend of youth and wisdom or you will soon lose any dynamic advantage you currently have.

Youth will always be the future. Is your future company attractive to them?

Here is my top ten list:

1. Demand and appeal for the products and services on offer.

Is there a demand for the products or services being offered by the company you are looking at? Look carefully at the facts presented. If there is a genuine current demand this will be verified by the company's sales figures.

Do the products and services appeal to you on a personal level? Would you be a customer of the company even if there was not a business opportunity attached?

The reason I ask this is I am trying to steer you towards the fact that when you have a totally authentic belief in your product or service, you will be very effective at taking your message about the product or service into the marketplace.

Next ask yourself this: how do you 'feel' about the product or service that is on offer? Feeling good about what you do is another invisible and intangible factor that becomes very visible when you start speaking with people. The people who believe in what they do and feel great about the service they offer can be spotted a mile off. They light up the room. Can you see yourself authentically telling others why your product, service or opportunity will make a difference in their lives?

Great companies rise and fall on great products and services so make sure you are rock solid on the detail of what you will be offering. Do not skip over this point and get seduced by the potential income you will make once your business is built. Without the combination of a solid product or service and market demand for it, whatever size business you build will not last long.

Many companies use authentic customer testimonials as evidence that their products or service creates the results they say. Take some time to read through these testimonials and where possible actually meet the individuals. I never fail to get inspired by the remarkable human stories of success despite all the odds that you come across on a daily basis in Network Marketing companies. There is no other industry, to the best of my knowledge, where customer results play such an integral part of communicating what is possible for the person who is considering the product or service on offer.

Try your best to be objective in your assessment of what is on offer. It's not easy. The persuasiveness of great product results combined with the evidence of what is possible for you are a highly motivational cocktail and so it should be.

Here is what I ask people to do: gather enough facts and make a decision after the emotion has passed. If you follow this advice you won't go far wrong. Instead of making any decisions in the heat of the moment, be strong and make your decisions once you have all the information you need on board. The reason I ask people to do this is because whatever they decide I want it to stick and be a permanent decision that they are happy with, even when things don't go perfectly to plan. Business is tough. There will always be ups and downs. That's just part of the world we are in. The last thing you want is a team running solely on emotions going up and down like a yoyo. Obviously life pulls people in all sorts of directions, so it's impossible to get everyone on track. Besides this, year on year I want our retention of people building the business to be as close to one hundred percent as possible. When you start people off based on the strong foundation of an educated decision, there is trust and professionalism. As a result, you are able to build on this over time by helping them develop the skills they need until they are ready to take full advantage of the opportunity you represent.

2. Customer care focused model.

We have all heard the phrase "The customer is King". Well guess what? They most definitely are. Without happy customers no business will survive. Truly successful Network Marketing business models that are totally focused on making sure their customers have an outstanding brand experience are making a huge step to being around for a long time. Putting customer care out there as your number one priority in all that you say and do makes a clear statement to the marketplace.

When your customers talk to their friends and family you need to make sure your service is part of their conversation. You want them to tell their friends and family that they feel valued, cared for and appreciated. I promise you, if you focus on this one thing people are going to stand up, listen and beat a path to your door.

We are living through dramatic changes in the way customers acquire goods and services. The age of the Internet has arrived. Instant information, price comparisons and next day delivery are just a few mouse clicks away. Friends of mine who run high street operations plus specialist retailers have seen their margins slashed as customers arrive with a print-out of someone offering the product they are after at a knockdown price. It leaves the retailer with very little room for manoever and certainly does not incentify them to add value to the customer experience.

Don't worry, it's not all gloom and doom. The very things that are driving thousands of established business to close their doors is also driving people in their millions towards Network Marketing distributors. Many of the products and services offered through Network Marketing companies are exclusively available from the distributors who represent the company you choose to get started with. While the company cannot fix the price, as this would be against the laws of free trade, it can certainly promote a culture of sticking to the recommended retail price as set by the parent company. This is how the majority of Network Marketing companies are able to protect the distributors' profit margin and thereby maintain the incentive for the distributor to offer outstanding added value to their customers.

As we illustrated earlier, when you compare Network Marketing with the conventional route to market there is a huge opportunity for people who want to be rewarded for focusing on customer care and customer follow-up. Especially when linked to a product or service that benefits from the added value of having someone explain how the product or service works.

The growth of online services has exploded and will continue to grow. In parallel with this growth is a growing body of people who remember what it was like to be cared for as a valued customer. They are happy to walk away from the automated "Have a nice day" emails in favour of the added value and personal service Network Marketing specialises in.

3. How much does their marketing plan pay out?

It's very important to know precisely how much income you will make for the efforts you put in. All of the leading companies in Network Marketing offer excellent up-front information to prospective business partners, so please study it carefully. Obviously products and services vary widely and the potential incomes and indirect commissions you are able to generate will depend on how they are offered to the marketplace.

The most important determination you need to make is whether or not you are after 'now money', 'future money' or both.

'Now money' is the instant money otherwise known as retail income you can create from day one by selling your product or service directly to your own customers. 'Future money', otherwise known as royalty or residual income, comes only after you have built and developed a team that services their own customers. This takes time and can often fluctuate dramatically until you have spent a number of years developing a solid, customer focused organisation full of experienced distributors.

Don't underestimate the importance of understanding these facts. Let me repeat this point because it's so easy to skim over this detail as you get dazzled by the bigger picture of where your life is heading. No matter how good you are, it will take time to develop a long term successful business. So you need to make sure you are financially able to survive the years where you will be investing time and money before earning any sizeable royalty based income.

Ask yourself a few simple questions once you have looked carefully at the payment plan proposed by your future company.

What is the average income being generated from people simply retailing the company's products and services?

Can you see yourself doing what others are doing in order to generate this income?

Can you see yourself doing more or less than others which allows you to estimate or project your potential level of income based on the average performance of others?

If you hit your targets (and it's a big if as you don't know yet) can you financially survive on the estimated income as your full-time wage?

Be careful. At this point don't confuse "believing in yourself" and simply being inexperienced. It's important to believe in yourself but it's equally important to make mature, informed decisions based on all the facts. Also, factor in the highs and lows of what can happen in everyday life. Things go wrong in our personal life that impact our business. Remember, I am trying to steer you towards creating financial independence and security so choose wisely.

Here is a better decision: if it's possible, start part-time with the security of your daytime job behind you. Build up your understanding of what's possible, with the safety net of knowing you will be ok if you have a few sticky months. As you build your confidence, experience and skills you can then plan when it's ok for you to sack your daytime boss and experience the freedom of running your own life.

4. Vision and professionalism of the management team.

No matter how good your product, service and company is, your efforts to develop long term financial security will be in vain without the security of knowing where your company is going.

Top of my list when assessing the character of the people who head your chosen company is to look at the mission statement, values and integrity that underpin its core message. I want to work with people who are the very best in their field and you should feel the same way. What do they stand for? How do they come across and what does their moral foundation look like? Are they professional, committed, community focused, family oriented and unselfish people? Or by contrast do they seem more like cut and thrust ruthless sales people trying to make fast money? This is your future and these are important questions.

Trust your instincts. What is the heartbeat of the company? Does it make you feel good or do you feel something is not quite right? Your instincts are very accurate but make sure you have enough facts at hand. Asses all the information available in a quiet space with no distractions. Once again, be careful. Don't allow your surface feelings and emotions to control the decision. They will fluctuate wildly. I am talking about how you feel deep down inside about the path you are about to take. If it feels right, it probably is right.

5. Brand projection, penetration and protection.

What does the brand you are about to represent project? Bear in mind this will soon be your brand. To succeed you will need to become the embodiment of its message. You will need to defend its position and shout it from the rooftops as if it was your personal creation. If people are going to trust the brand and its message they will look at you and how much you fully embrace the product or service you represent.

Over and over we have said that people are looking for belief and confidence. For them to acquire that from you they will want to know that you believe in your company one hundred percent. Then and only then can they borrow this belief and use it to propel their personal confidence.

Next, look at how deep your brand can penetrate society. Does it appeal to everyone or is there a small target audience? Knowing the size of your target market will help you to consider the viability of your plans. Will the market you are going after provide you with enough opportunity?

Lastly, brand protection. Does your future company have robust and secure rules and regulations to stop anyone from misrepresenting your brand? Having something that's valuable also means you need a strong legal framework to protect your asset. Does the company have all the appropriate documentation and processes in place to ensure you and your activity are protected in every way possible?

6. Momentum of the company: local, national and international.

Joining a company that has momentum can have a significant impact on your chances. Look at the company statements and look at the headline sales growth being experienced in different areas. If sales figures are increasing it means there is a group of people effectively taking the company's message to the market place.

Timing is everything in business. If you catch a company during a sweet spot of growth your efforts will be supported and multiplied by the confidence of those around you. This confidence affects your thinking and subsequently the thinking of your team and their customers. This makes the day-to-day things you do to advance your business seem easier, which means you work harder and gain more success. It just becomes a self-perpetuating machine.

By contrast, if you join a company during a downward trend in its growth it can be hard when your excitement and enthusiasm is not matched by the people you meet. Distributors are unsure of their actions and they are searching for a way forward. Confidence is replaced with doubt and the decisive actions of yesterday are replaced by indecision and procrastination.

In the title it says: "local, national and international". Identifying precisely what region of a large business is actually experiencing momentum is also important. You can be in a country where the company overall is doing great but locally the leadership may be flat. That's when it's important to travel to where the excitement is, as I explained earlier in the book, with our international fact finding trips.

Use social media to connect with and develop friendships with the teams moving up in your company. As you develop your communication, look into which areas are within driving distance and are currently doing well. Work with your team-mates and build bridges with the people in these areas. Ask them if you can travel to look into what they are doing better than everyone else. It's essential that you form the same habits as the people who are getting ahead and be sure not to copy any of the bad practices being applied by local leaders who may have lost their momentum.

If it's needed, use the carrot that you will do all you can to help them in your area as their team expands because few people will do something for nothing.

The last but probably the most important factor about momentum is to understand that you are the very person who creates it. If it's not there it's down to you to make it happen.

Great companies are made great by the people who pick up the flag and fly it better than anyone else around them. I have seen so many companies that have been bumping along, catch fire and fly just because a small group of like-minded people decided to say now is the time. In the twenty-five years I have spent in the amazing industry, momentum has ebbed and flowed based on all of these factors many times.

If success was as easy as finding a company that's really flying and just parking your surf board on their wave then everyone would do this. Don't be that naive. Even if you join a company that's doing really well, if a bunch of the leaders that are driving the growth slide into sunbathing mode you will quickly see the growth trend slow down. At this point weak distributors say: "What's wrong with the company? What's wrong with the marketplace? I wish it was like the old days when it was easy." etc. There is nothing wrong with the company or the marketplace. A few key people took their foot off the gas which they are allowed to do and production slows down. It's that simple. If new leaders fail to step up to the plate as the old guard takes a rest, then doubt will set in.

If you or anyone else wants what others have already achieved then you have to roll up your sleeves and put the work in. When you accept and adopt this approach you will develop your own personal momentum and become unstoppable.

7. Long term stability of the company.

Without a degree in accountancy, economics and international management, it's pretty difficult for you as a newbie to analyse the long term viability of the company you want to join. Don't worry. Even stock market analysts with all the resources at their fingertips get it wrong when it comes to assessing the potential for growth of many companies, so let me give you a few tips.

Obviously it goes without saying that brand new startup companies are going to present the highest risk but equally they can present very dynamic exciting opportunities. The 'now money', as described earlier which many of the startup companies will focus you on, can be very attractive. But be careful they are not over hyping the potential earnings. Plus, you need to factor into your decision that new companies can be unstable for all sorts of reasons, so choose wisely with that knowledge on board.

If you are looking for the safer route, choose from one of the large established companies that have been around for a long time. They are carefully audited each year so you can have a fair degree of confidence in their predictions. Some would have literally billions at risk if their plans were not extremely well thought through, so they are highly likely to continue on the path to further growth.

They may not represent the most exciting route like some of the startups but they do offer long term stability and that's a hugely important factor when building for the future. Look at all parties' predictions and plans and ask yourself if they are aligned with your personal ambitions. If they are then you have made a good choice.

8. Training and support online and offline.

All of the leading companies offer outstanding online and offline training and support. Years and years of trial and error, practice and refinement have led to slick processes in all the established companies. Naturally the new startup companies learn from the giants of the industry, so there can be no excuse for you not receiving outstanding support at the very point when you need it most.

The Internet has been a revelation in how Network Marketing companies exchange information with their distributors. It has vastly improved the speed of communication and the quality of training the companies are able to share with their often home-based distributors.

Online methods range from step by step website pages, dedicated YouTube channels, live and recorded webinars and much more. Social media platforms such as Facebook, Twitter, WhatsApp and Pinterest have exploded the distributors' ability to reach huge audiences. The same platforms are also used for instant recognition, guidance and notification on all sorts of subjects through the myriad of group chats you are able to set up.

Offline you can participate in one to one detailed instruction sessions, small group gatherings in people's homes or offices, weekly hotel meetings and full blown monthly seminars with hundreds of people.

Quarterly or half yearly, in addition to the above more localised events, you may have the opportunity to attend bigger events with thousands of people. Often these events are held at major venues around the country. There can also be glamorous parties attached, giving the leading distributors a chance to meet the up and coming future distributors that will have hit a sales volume target to be there. This trims the audience down to only the most serious people. This is where you get a chance to rub shoulders with the most successful distributors in your company and as such should not be missed at any cost.

Although you will have many exciting ideas you will want to test drive, be sure to follow the tried and tested methods established by the hard work and millions of hours invested by those distributors who have gone before you. In the vast majority of cases there is no need to reinvent the wheel. It's simply a matter of studying what works best and putting in the appropriate effort required.

9. Collaboration between leadership.

Look at the mindset of the team you are thinking of joining or are already involved with. If you are lucky enough to be guided by mature leaders they will fully appreciate and apply the laws and benefits to adopting a collaborative leadership approach to everything.

Collaborative leaders reach out and build bridges at every opportunity with other leaders. They understand a rising tide raises all ships. They are always focused on the bigger picture of helping everyone succeed. They do this with the knowledge and confidence that understands the more success we can all point to, the greater the possibilities are for everyone.

These visionary leaders as are not governed by land grab mentality. They understand there is enough room for everyone to succeed. They are not driven by a scarcity mentality. They have abundance thinking and know they will need a wide range of input and support if their ambitions are to be fully realised. They are not trying to selfishly protect their own little patch. They know that by reaching out and forming relationships that help and support others, they will receive the same support in return for themselves and their organisation.

Working together with the management of your company and the other leaders will allow you to create a framework of support that when built correctly will look after your whole organisation as it expands. By sharing responsibility to create this platform you also open your team up to the wider understanding of what is possible for them. The more examples they see, the more personalities they are exposed to and the more they begin to believe what they can achieve.

As the integration grows, everyone recognises they are part of one big team and they pull together. Every weakness is covered by the collective efforts of the team working towards one common goal. As this happens, individual leaders experience a level of freedom that would never happen if they had tried to succeed on their own.

Make it your ambition to be this type of leader. Set the example for your team as they watch you unselfishly help others at every opportunity. Do this and your organisation will develop into the service driven professionals they need to be and continue the legacy of being flag bearers for this great industry.

10. Can you work part-time or full-time?

Lastly, can you work your new venture part-time or do you have to commit full-time? This question is important on the basis of what you actually want for your life. Remember you are the one calling the shots now, so you need to decide what the priorities are for the life you want to live.

Some people are happy to commit huge amounts of their time to a new venture while others are looking for more freedom or flexibility than they can get from their present situation.

There will be many factors that dictate the answer to that question so consider them all and decide on a plan for yourself. The company you are looking at may be a rare example and offer you an outstanding full-time opportunity that suits your needs from day one. If it offers you the income potential and security you need within the hours that suit you and you have checked every single detail of what to expect, then take the plunge and go for it. That's pretty unusual though, so be careful.

Most companies will offer you the chance to start off as a self-employed entrepreneur and provide no guarantee of income at all. You are not in a job situation where you can expect a wage packet no matter what. You are in business for yourself now. Do nothing and you get nothing. Do lots and you can earn lots. It's exciting and scary all at the same time.

That's why I suggest you start part-time and minimise any risk. There is no reason to put yourself under any pressure. Build part-time. Switch off the TV or any other distractions. Learn all you can as fast as you can. It's amazing what can happen.

CHAPTER 9

YOUR FIRST YEAR
IN NETWORK MARKETING.

CHAPTER 9

Your first year in Network Marketing.

Building and developing your own Network Marketing business in my opinion is one of the most exciting projects you will ever get involved in. Billionaires and businessmen all across the world point to it as one of the best ways forward for anyone considering a career as an entrepreneur.

I know distributors who spend just a few weeks in Network Marketing then quit and walk away. I know distributors whose self-belief limits them to making one hundred pounds per month. I know distributors who have replaced professional salaries and are happy to work from home earning over ten thousand pounds per month, and I know distributors who have learned to take away all their limitations and make over one million pounds per year. Only you can decide where you fit in.

In this chapter I am going to cover all of the most important elements in getting your business off to a great start. If you fully understand its potential you are destined for some sleepless nights.

As you contemplate the possibility of starting out on your own, please understand that the limitations on what you can and will achieve will only be controlled by you. Add to this the millions of testimonials of those who have gone before you and it becomes an intoxicating mix. So what can go wrong?

Let's deal with the negatives first.

There is a strange phenomenon that happens to almost everyone who decides to get started in Network Marketing. In one way, shape or another, some of the people around you who have never previously mentioned business suddenly become experts on what you are about to do and can't wait to share their opinions with you.

Friends, family and loved ones are the very people you would expect to support your new decision most but for some strange reason it does not always work out that way. Our confidence is fragile in the first year and we want more than anything for people to believe in what we do. When some of our nearest and dearest don't believe in us, or worse still they hurt our feelings with ill-informed opinions, it's easy to feel a little offended and over-react to even the slightest criticism.

Learning not to get drawn into energy zapping conversations, being mentally tough and sticking to the facts as opposed to being overly emotional with your responses are just a few of the many skills you will need to navigate these choppy waters.

Read on and I will explain the actual reasons why some people may doubt your new venture. Some of the reasons will surprise you. When you understand these reasons it will help to reinforce in your mind that you have actually made a great decision.

You stop transferring any of the doubt into your own expectations and begin the process of not needing any external validation of the path you have chosen. It's pointless getting into an argument over who is right or wrong. I will give you some easy-to-follow strategies to avoid these issues.

Lastly, I will encourage you to recognise that not everyone will be happy for your success. That's just how life is. Sadly there are some relationships that you simply have to walk away from. In time you will see the real benefits of this.

Getting off to a great start.

Wherever you are right now, this chapter will help you focus on all the time-tested, basic steps that Network Marketing leaders take to supercharge their business. There is a lot to learn in any new venture but I am confident that you can apply all of the steps I am about to teach you. New people often get themselves in a tangle as they wrestle with their exciting new career. Follow my advice and you will avoid most of the mistakes I see on a daily basis.

If you are still harbouring a little self-doubt (which many people do) here is yet another bit of good news: it's not the end of the world if you don't get off to a great start.

Your Network Marketing career allows you to make as many mistakes as you need to make until you get to a point where you say enough is enough, I am ready and want to make this work. When you reach that point, draw a line under the past and make a fresh start. Tomorrow may be the first day that you are able to put all your ideas together and really begin to create the momentum you deserve.

Start off with the end in mind.

Before you get started, write down all that you want to achieve in your new career opportunity. Have clear and definitive goals of the amount of money you want to earn and the changes you want to make to your lifestyle as a result of the income and freedom you intend to create

It's vital that you know *why* you are committed to your new venture. When you take time to know why, you will definitely work out *how* you're going to put it all together. Take some time over this. Write everything down. Every single super-achiever in the world does this and you will be no different.

Revisit Chapter 6 on the benefits of Network Marketing and be sure to set short, mid and long term goals. Use your company manual combined with the testimonials of others who have gone before you and pretty quickly you will build up a road map of what you want to achieve.

Design a business that serves your goals.

We all have different goals. I love to paint and enjoy nature and I hated being trapped in a job, so freedom was big on my priority list as opposed to making money for any material things. Here is an example of what I wrote for myself when getting started.

"My business has allowed me to sack my boss, be time and money free, to travel the world doing what I want, when I want and it feels fantastic."

Another priority was for me to surround myself with top quality, fun people. I knew I wanted my future children to grow up in a positive, uplifting environment. So I made lists of all the qualities I wanted my team to have. Going forward, every time I spoke to people I told them about the list I had and was amazed at how many people not only wanted to live up to the qualities I was asking for, they were inspired by them and created lists of their own.

Here are some of the qualities I insist people have and or develop in order to be part of the team.

All of the people around me are kind, compassionate, grateful, hardworking, fun-loving, solution oriented, happy and friendly. They love music, art and nature. It feels fantastic to be around them". Go ahead and create your own list.

Become the person who represents all of the qualities on your list and you will attract the same people into your life. Simple.

Be sure to create exactly the business and the life that you want!

I needed to create a business that operated with our without me.

Far too many people new to Network Marketing introduce customers and distributors who they feel they need to constantly look after. This is a mistake. That type of business offers no freedom and is not what I propose you create.

From the start, let people know that you will show them all the basics they need to support their success but ultimately it's down to them and how hard they want to work.

This point is critical. Too many people feel that baby-sitting their team will lead to success. Trust me, the opposite is true. Of course there are many other support mechanisms I will encourage you to utilise in the development of your business but it's essential you do not create a business that solely depends on you.

Teach your team to use all the training tools at their disposal while you continue to introduce people personally. Eighty percent of your time should be used for building new business and twenty percent of your time should be used for managing the business you have already created. They can get everything else they need from the parent company, distributor meetings and social media, freeing you up to grow a bigger business.

Teach the teachers to teach the teachers to teach and you will be free!

Align yourself with the mission of your chosen company.

Make sure you are crystal clear on the mission of your company. There is nothing more powerful than a distributor who is the perfect example of everything their company stands for. Read and study everything you can get your hands on. Understand that your customers' and your teams' belief and confidence will be in direct proportion to your own belief and confidence, so take time to absorb every little detail.

The more you learn the more you will earn, it's that simple. As your competence grows the marketplace sees you and your company as one entity. As opposed to working for a company you *are* the company. It becomes part of you and your identity. Do all of these things and you will make yourself the go-to person in your area.

Study the old and the new people in your company.

Within every company there are two groups of people to study: the established, successful distributors who have been around for years and the distributors who are new, hungry, on the move and destined for the top.

There will be lots to learn from both groups but you have to be careful. Leaders can be very charismatic and persuasive. If they are moving ahead and building a long term sustainable business model focused on customer care, it's a fair bet they are on track and you will be well advised to listen to what they have to say. If they are out of production and purely reliant on stories about the glory days of the past, be careful.

The older, established leaders represent all that is possible and as such deserve a high level of respect and appreciation for being the trail blazers in your chosen company. These are people who were once in the very same position as you but with little or no success to point to. They believed in the future of the company, conquered their fears, built their confidence and skills and one step at a time put their business together.

They will have wonderful, inspiring stories to tell on how they achieved this. So my advice is to listen intently and take great notes. Learning from someone else's experience in the same career can save you many hours of work. Focus on the principles and core values they feel are important to building a long sustainable business and be sure to apply what you learn to your business as it grows.

As you listen to these stories, look carefully at the history of your company. Look at how it has evolved along with the distributors who helped to build its foundations and look at where it's going. All of these elements are important.

If companies are going to survive and thrive they have to constantly adapt and change. The same goes for staying current as a leader in the marketplace. Established leaders can sometimes get stuck in the past and be resistant to change. Be aware of this and be sure that you are following someone who is bang up-to-date with all of the latest ways to penetrate the marketplace.

In contrast to the polished, refined and established leaders there will be another group of leaders in your chosen company and these are the ones you need to run with. They will be bursting with energy, innovative and driven to get to the top with a 'no matter what' attitude.

Model yourself and your actions on the up and coming top achievers.

Look for people who are passionate about the mission and direction of the company and are getting serious results in the current marketplace.

Do not underestimate the power of who you associate with. "Birds of a feather flock together" and without any doubt "winners run with winners". Go out of your way to build friendships with these new leaders. Find out what they do and mirror their actions as carefully as you can. Network Marketing is a game of duplication. It's rare that you have to completely reinvent the wheel, so park your opinion and just copy what is getting great results for the current flock of leaders.

In time you will be able to match everything they say but deliver your information with your own personality. Before long you will find yourself talking fluently about everything you and your company stand for and it will feel amazing. Practice, study, practice, study, practice, study, over and over and you will get better and better. Pretty soon hesitation and fear will disappear forever. Day-to-day tasks become second nature and that's where the fun begins. You're on your way to the top and only you can stop you.

Master the basic skills.

In every industry and every company there are always four or five basic skills to master that will allow you to climb to the top. Network Marketing is no different.

Here are four classics that you need to work on until they become second nature. Imagine, just four things to master and you can build a business that can propel you into the top one percent earning bracket of the country.

Honestly, it amazes me even today that new starters don't fully take this on board. Decide here and now to become the best you can be at these simple tasks and I promise you there will be no upper limit to what you can achieve.

The four classics that determine growth.

LIPS: List. Invite. Present. Support.

List the people you know right now and the people you have not met.

One of the worst feelings in the world is to be bursting with excitement about what you want to communicate and have nobody to talk to. Don't let that happen to you.

Within your company manual there will be simple but very effective guidelines on how to get your list started. Please follow these tips carefully and decide to be a master list builder.

The bigger your list the greater your confidence will be that you can find customers and distributors for your new project. Don't prejudge anyone. Put everyone on your list. The truth is that your warm market list is just the beginning. Think of the list off the list, i.e. who do you know? Then who do they know? Then who do they know? There are billions of people on this planet. Learn the skill of list building and you will have a limitless resource to work from.

Professional Networkers master the art of making new contacts every day, everywhere they go. Master this art and your list will always be growing.

Put yourself into environments where you meet people. Be professional about it. Make plans. Take it a step further and go to places where the target audience will be suited to the people you are looking for.

If there was one thing I wish I had done from day one, this is it: I wish I had put every contact I ever made and every customer onto a categorised email data base and sent them an appropriate email once a month just letting them know I am here to serve them whenever they need me. Simple to do and simple not to do.

There is no need to pester people but there is every need to let them know you are still there. Otherwise your initial hard work will be in vain and they will become someone else's customer or distributor. It's never too late to start. Apply this simple rule to your life and you will be amazed at how effective it is. Within a few years that list can be in the thousands. With the miracle of automated email platforms such as Mail Chimp and Constant Contact, you can stay in contact and show how professional you are about following people up for life.

Professional Networkers understand the importance of the list and work on theirs every single day. Creating a pipeline of never-ending contacts to present your product or opportunity to will allow you to keep refining your skills and ultimately keep expanding your business.

There are many books on how to build lists and I recommend you get your hands on a few and study all the techniques available on how to do this.

Building your list and reach using social media platforms.

This is without doubt one of the most exciting ways to build a big audience but equally it can be a huge distraction that consumes your time. It can and will be a costly mistake if you are not careful.

Firstly, let me be clear. It's impossible to cover this topic at length in this book and give it the airtime it deserves. All I am going to do is prompt you to learn more and decide how you are going to weave it into your business.

Social media is here to stay. If you are fortunate enough to be young, that's a no-brainer for you but you still need to learn how to use it and harness its power.

If you are older you may see social media as more of an intrusion on your time and question its worth. Please do not put your head in the sand at this point. If you don't study and become competent with using it, I can assure you your competitors will. You have been warned.

Here are some of the things social media will allow you to do with respect to your business development.

The good:

It can help you establish your brand identity.

It can help you reach massive audiences and build huge lists.

It can help you interact and develop relationships that would be impossible without it.

It can help you share content and training material with individuals or specific groups.

It can dramatically increase your time efficiency.

Used in the wrong way the bad looks like this:

It can ruin your brand identity.

It can damage massive audiences and trash your list.

It can destroy interaction and development of relationships.

It can help you share the wrong content and training material with individuals or specific groups.

It can dramatically decrease your time efficiency.

Watching videos of dogs in Superman costumes, ice bucket challenges, cute kids dancing for their families, etc. will not help you get rich! So, as you can appreciate it's important you get it right.

And that's the tip of the iceberg.

Facebook, Linked-In, Twitter, WhatsApp, Pinterest, etc. are all growing at a mind-bending rate and you cannot ignore this.

They all have excellent tips, advice and guidelines on how to set up and get the best from their platforms. They are a dream come true for anyone looking to build, educate, train and inspire a group of people. Just a little Google research will bring you up to speed on each one but please be careful, you can waste lots of time and energy interacting with people in a fashion that will not advance your business. Each have their own idiosyncrasies that you will need to get used to but once you master them, as the lists above indicate, they can and will have a huge impact on your business.

If you are just starting out, don't try to activate everything at once. Start off with whichever platform you feel comfortable with and then expand from there. Eventually, as you look to be more organised and time efficient you can use platforms like Hootsuite and many others. They allow you to automate your posting and interaction with all the leading providers and pretty soon you will be on your way to global domination of the airwaves.

And finally, please don't become a social media bore. Respect the dynamics of social media. Of course you can share your business, its products and the fact that you are excited about your life but make sure there is a healthy mixture and balance. 'Social' media; there is a clue in the title.

People love to offer their opinions so be prepared for some unwanted feedback. Protect your brand. Be professional. Be polite. Never air your laundry in public. Block or delete any unwanted people and use the private message option whenever personal conversations are needed.

Keep your experience fun and light. Be careful not to waste too much time getting distracted by the enormous amount of content you can access.

Remember, this is about building your list, so stay focused.

And finally, just a few words on how to follow up the list you have built.

If you build a massive audience list but fail to talk to them then they don't know you exist. Learn to stay in touch with outstanding copy content. As I stated earlier, people don't want to get pestered but they do like to know they have some positive options there for them when they are ready.

Please remember to focus on what they want. Look at the New Year resolutions each year. They never change. Most people want to lose weight, get into the best shape of their life, drop a few pounds before summer, make more money, find a rewarding career, get out of debt, etc.

Whatever product you represent, list all the main motivating influences that will get people engaged with your product or opportunity and compose them into some banging strap lines. Once you know what they are it's just a matter of keeping your message current, in front of your list and looking as sharp as possible.

Don't forget it's about always adding value and personalising your message. When you write do it in a simple, easy to understand and friendly conversation manner. There is no need to be perfect but there is every need to be you. Don't dazzle them with all you know and how clever you are. Just be nice.

Let them know you care and you're looking forward to helping them when they are ready and don't waffle. Keep it short and snappy.

Always include a strong call to action with an added promotional benefit to acting now. For example: "Contact me before (state date) and you will get (bonus item) extra for this limited period of time."

Don't make it all about the sale. Sign up for information feeds that you can use from your company or other sources that validate what you offer and weave that in also.

Once you have it all set out, top and tail it with great testimonials and you're done. BOOM! That's called building a list and staying in touch with it.

Invite.

Learning how to deliver a simple and effective invitation to look at your product, service or business opportunity is essential.

Before I give you some simple, easy-to-learn scripts, let me make a few observations that you will need to respect and appreciate.

People buy people. What this really means is people buy from or listen to people they like. So be likeable. Don't be over-bearing, flashy or pushy. There really is no need to be. It's not about you and your performance, it's about them and how you can help them. Understand what you are going to do. You are going to communicate some information about what you do and what you represent. If they want what you have then great. If they don't that's great also. It's just a matter of going through the numbers to find out who wants what you have.

At all costs, avoid coming across as a slick salesperson. Otherwise, your prospect is likely to run a mile. People hate to be sold to but people love to buy. If you just focus on making the sale and the answer is no, then that's the end of your opportunity to convert them. If you focus on building a relationship first above all else, even if now is not the time for them, they will remember how friendly you were and the fact that you did not try to push anything on them. As a result there is every chance they will come back to you in the future.

Once you have these sentiments on board the invite becomes very easy.

Please trust me. I have read, tested and absorbed all the leading theories on which sales scripts are the best. I have one of the biggest book collections of any leader I have met and treat nothing casually. It's not about the perfection of the script. It's about you, your passion, your enthusiasm and your belief in what can happen for them and that's it.

Please stick to what I type for now. I have seen so many people change a few words here and there because they feel they know better and end up delivering a totally different impression.

If I say to my wife: "Deb. When I look into your eyes the hands of time stand still", I am in for a good night. If I change that a little and say: "Deb. You have a face that would stop a clock", I am in trouble. I hope you get my point?

Having said that, obviously the script is just a basic outline. It still has to fit you and your personality, so feel free to chat naturally but please respect some of the tips and boundaries I offer.

Just a few more last-minute things. You are trying to line up the appointment to deliver a presentation, not actually deliver the presentation. So at all costs please avoid trying to explain your offer over the phone.

Last but not least, smile when on the phone. I have no idea why but when you smile you feel and sound happy. Happy people are attractive, so smile big!

Simple invite to Circle of Influence:

You: "Hi Mary. It's John here."

COI: "Hi John. How are you?"

You: "Hope the kids, the dogs etc. are good. (Blah, blah...)".

"Hey Mary, listen. The reason I called is that I have some information I want to share with you. It won't take you long to go through it. If I send it over will you study it?"

COI: "What's it all about?"

You: "It's too much to cover over the phone. It's easier if I send you the link but I just want to make sure you go through it. Is that ok?"

COI: "Yes. Ok."

You: "Great! I will send it over tonight. Drop me a line or call as soon as you have looked at it. I will give you a call tomorrow if you don't ring back tonight."

Most companies have online content so I just used the word "link" above. Please adapt the pitch if you only have offline materials.

Look; the bottom line is this: if they are looking, they are looking. If they are not, they are not but it's important you find out either way. This is not a sales pitch.

Of course, I could write pages on the perfect things to say and how to handle any objections that come your way. But again, experience teaches me to just stick to your guns and repeat the following sentence.

"Honestly, it's too complicated to explain over the phone, so I would prefer to send you a link. Is that ok?"

Some people waste days, weeks, months or even years believing they're not quite perfect, so they avoid making the calls. That's crazy. This is just about sharing information with the market place and allowing the right people to step forward.

The critical detail is your posture. Know that you don't need to be word perfect. Know that you don't need them to say yes. Know that it's you doing them the favour. Know what you have is potentially of great value to them. Know you are going to succeed with or without them (without ever saying it) and know there will be lots more calls to make no matter what they say, so make the call!

Hey, tennis is a great sport but it's not for everyone. Golf is a great sport but it's not for everyone. I enjoy a nice steak now and then but my vegetarian friends think I am crazy. Each to their own. Some will, some won't, so what, who's next.

Now I think that's pretty simple. It's not who you speak to, it's how many you speak to.

Speak to a few and you make a little money. Speak to loads and you make lots of money! I loved that when I first heard it and I still love it today.

Finally, having covered what to say and what not to say, let me assure you that you can't say the wrong thing to the right person. As I have just stated, don't wait to be perfect. You never will be. If the person you are talking to wants your product, service or opportunity they will say yes even if you are terrible.

You are looking for people who are looking for what you offer. You are not looking for people who need to be sold on making a decision. At the end of the day it's that simple, so speak to more people.

Present.

Once you have the prospect's attention by sharing some advance information (it saves so much time and effort if you can do this), now it's time to deliver an effective presentation.

Learning to present your product and opportunity in a fashion that is enjoyable and easy for your prospects to process is critical. Pretty much all the questions that you will be asked will have been asked before, so please take time to learn all the standard answers.

Whether you use PowerPoint, pen and paper or state-of-the-art online videos and web pages, essentially people buy people.

Life is a show and people want to have fun and be entertained. I am not asking you to be a comedian but don't be too serious. Of course, building a business and pursuing success is a serious subject but please be careful, people are attracted to happy people, so smile, enjoy yourself and just make a friend.

Here are my basic formulae. Again, no miracles just a nice, simple way to be around people with the sincere understanding that they will want what you have if your product or service fulfils their needs.

Believe in who you are, what you do and be sure to enjoy yourself.

Put the person opposite you at ease as soon as possible.

It's important that whoever you are presenting to do not feel you are going to try and give them the big sales pitch, so cover this at the start.

Just be natural, relaxed and honest with them. Intelligent people only make serious decisions that last after collecting enough facts. So understand that you're there just to share some information.

What I say once the basic greetings and a little small talk are over varies but essentially you just need a few words to trigger you to start. Use your own words if you want but please get to the point. Don't waffle.

"Mary. It's great to see you and I'm glad we could find time to meet.

You will be glad to know I am not going to try and sell you anything. All I am going to do is run through some information that I think you are going to find really interesting, then you can ask some questions. Sound ok?

One more thing. As I go through this information, think about other people it may be perfect for. Think about anyone you know who could be looking for an additional income or change of career."

And that's it. You're away. Keep it fun and simple at all costs.

Every company has its own culture of how to present their products and services so study all the presentation materials and follow the recommendations carefully.

Ask the top-achieving distributors if you can tape them doing all the basic presentations that you will need to duplicate. Study what they do. Copy them as carefully as you can but always remember to keep everything fun and simple.

Support.

Support takes commitment and your fledgling business will need a lot of care and attention. Much like a farmer tends his crops after planting. Just like a parent watches over a baby until they become an adult. It's what you do once your new customer or distributor relationship has been established that will define your future in this great industry.

Understanding that relationships need to be developed and nurtured over time can be difficult concepts for young, dynamic and sometimes impatient distributors to embrace. I remember being twenty-three like it was yesterday. I wish someone had shared these points with me when I got started. It would have saved so much frustration.

It's easy to look at people and agree with society's view of who they are and where their place might be. It takes genuine love, leadership and vision to look beyond the surface and see who they can be. Given the right environment, people can change and become so much more. Be one of those people who gives someone a chance. Believe in them when nobody else does and you will be surprised at how good it makes you feel. Of course I don't want you to be naive or gullible. Protect your boundaries and never put yourself in dangerous situations but just sending a message to someone saying that you think they can become more may be the catalyst they need, so give it a try.

The people you work with are going to make a lot of mistakes. Some of these human errors are going to hurt you and hurt you deeply. Occasionally you will be confused. You won't have the tools to deal with some of the complex ways that people can make you feel about who you are. Don't worry. Over time you will learn to deal with all of these issues and grow stronger as a result of every test you go through. In simple terms you are going to need to forgive people and you are going to need to forgive yourself. Make that a part of your plan and you will take a big step to lightening your load.

Over time your emerging team picks up on these characteristics and the foundation of your business becomes a strong, reliable experience that allows you to expand and grow. Everyone understands that their role is to care for their customers more than they care for themselves and your whole organisation pushes ahead as one team.

The journey of understanding the human psyche is fascinating and rewarding beyond belief. If you want to be a top achiever in any industry, make this your top priority.

Your fortune will be a direct reflection of how you care for people. It's that simple.

ATTACK.

There are many different acronyms you can use. I like 'ATTACK' because it puts me in an action mindset. It quickly focuses my mind on the main objectives that need attention each day.

Attract. Train. Teach. Activate. Congratulate. Kind and patient.

Attract.

Becoming an attractive person needs to be your number one priority.

Attracting people to you and your mission will be a massive part of your success. Who you are, what you do, what you represent and how you portray yourself will determine how attractive other people find you.

When people are attracted to you and your product you have an opportunity to engage with them and share the benefits of your product and opportunity.

Attraction is the opposite of pursuing people, so think carefully about the messages both obvious and subliminal that you send into the marketplace. Look at people you admire. Look at people who are successful within your environment and make sure you mirror the attractive qualities they project into the marketplace.

Train.

Your company will have excellent training materials, so be sure to promote and utilise them for yourself and within your team. Get on track as soon as possible.

To succeed in this arena you want your actions to be as easy to learn from and copy as possible. Start off with training yourself to keep everything very simple and duplicatable.

The dream reaction you are always looking for is: "Waw, that looks simple. I think I can do that." Better still is: "Waw, that looks simple. I think I can do that. In fact I think I can do it better than you!"

You may be surprised to learn that most new people genuinely get started with an ambition to impress people with their presentations. Please trust me. This is not the X-Factor. It's not about being impressive, it's about showing people that anyone can do what you do. The last thing you want to do is be too impressive. You don't want your team saying: "Waw, that looks great, amazing. But I don't think I can ever be as good as you."

I hope that takes the pressure off a little.

Double and triple check you are on track and getting results from the actions you take in your early days because your team will blindly copy what they see you do. "Monkey see, monkey do" is very much the watchword. Learn to self-study. Examine each detail of your activity and seek to improve one little step at a time.

As you get better, share your experience with your customers and your team. Let people know you were less than perfect when you started. People love to learn from other people's stories.

Teach.

Teaching is more personal than just training someone. You have to guide people step by step. As your team experience small victories, confidence and belief builds. So be sure to break everything down into small achievable pieces.

One of the classic mantras that I use over and over is: Tell. Show. Try. Do.

Tell people what they need to do. Show people what to do. Get them to try and then stay in touch with them until they do what they need to do.

This approach allows the new person to hear, see and feel each step of getting their new business off the ground. If you want to learn to swim you have to get in the water. The sooner you get yourself and your new people into action the less time fear or indecision has a chance to set in. So jump in and go for it.

Activate.

You can spend as long as you want talking about doing something but at some point you have to take action. Successful people take decisive action once they have the basic facts on board and then learn from the outcome.

Unsuccessful people take forever to make up their mind about getting into production and then when they eventually start they change their mind quickly.

The best way to create action is to have a huge sense of urgency as we have already discussed. So don't underestimate the power of knowing what you dreams really are. Look at them again and again until they become a burning ambition. Once you are committed to your "why", I promise you the "how" will come automatically.

Congratulate.

Congratulate your customers and your team at every opportunity. Taking time to recognise people with little messages, cards, flowers, cakes or champagne will make a big difference. Sounds old-fashioned doesn't it? It is and people love it. Showing you care and are prepared to show it sets you apart from other people who make it all business.

People need to feel appreciated, loved and occasionally important. Don't miss a chance to let them know you value them.

Recognition is everything. Soldiers die for it and children cry for it. Make it a part of what you do each day.

Kind and patient.

Successful businesses are built on relationships that grow over time. It's so important to be kind and patient. Let new people find their feet. I cannot overstate these principles.

Network Marketing is all about customer care and helping people grow and develop as human beings. It's rare for people to have a perfectly honed skill set from day one. It's going to take an awful lot of trial and error, failure and disappointment before you and your superstars earn their stripes. You want to be seen as a supportive influence in their lives.

One of my favorite sentences sums it all up perfectly: "People don't care how much you know until they know how much you care."

Some more points that also help to make a big difference.

Time management.

As we discussed in Chapter 7, learn to compress time. Less is always more. Once you have learned all the basics it will then be down to how many people you are presenting to. How efficient you are at getting your message across can be as simple as taking a presentation from thirty minutes to fifteen minutes and having ten in the room as opposed to one. The more people you present to, the faster you will grow.

Team spirit and the greenhouse effect.

Great leaders create great team spirit. It's not enough to belong to just the company team. Emerging groups need someone to be the ground breaker and that needs to be you. Raise the bar in all you do and look to create the best formula for growth.

The greenhouse effect (glasshouse, if American) will maximise your returns. Plants grow through difficult winters because the greenhouse protects and looks after them when they are at their most fragile. Make sure your developing team is carefully nurtured in a similar personal development greenhouse culture of meetings, conference calls, social media groups and anything else that can stop them from being out in the cold on their own.

Promotion of meetings and the bigger picture.

Learn to promote the bigger picture for people. Whether you realise it or not, people initially judge your company through you. As quickly as possible show them other people and what they have achieved, allowing them to form a perspective from a wider picture. It's essential they get as many frames of reference as possible that prove to them that anyone can succeed, including them. Do this and they will struggle to find excuses not to get serious.

Learn how to be a master promoter.

There are promoters and there are promoters. Personally I am going to pitch the next event like the person's life depends on it. The truth is it may well do. Time and again I have seen someone dragged kicking and screaming into an event and then BOOM! The lights go on, they realise what they can achieve and overnight their life explodes into a world of possibilities.

Do all you can to get your people to the next event or onto the next piece of information. You have to believe in their future more than they do. Here is my favourite phrase in helping someone make a decision. Remember I want to help them and I want to work with them so here it is:

You: "Do you trust me?"

Them: "Yes."

You: "Are you sure you trust me?"

Them: "Yes."

You: "Then great! If you truly do, you will come to the next event."

It's that simple. When they attend they will realise what a fine line it was in not coming and they will be extremely grateful. Everyone I have ever taken to an event has enjoyed themselves. Put another way, if they go they grow. If they don't they won't.

"Sorry Mary. I can't help you if you are not going to trust me and take action!" Simple.

Events are key to people seeing the big picture of what is possible.

Edification of the people helping you.

One of the simplest ways to get your team to want to meet the people helping you is to speak highly of them. Don't look for the glory and the spotlight.

Just tell your team you are having such amazing support that your success is almost guaranteed. When you speak like this it's inevitable that the serious people in your team will want to meet your mentors.

When they eventually meet them your mentors get a chance to tell your team how amazing you are and all of a sudden your team starts to listen to you. Another simple thing that works like a dream. Easy to do and easy not to do.

What if you fall out with your personal mentors?

This happens from time to time. It's a people business and people disagree sometimes. Let's talk about alternative pathways if things go wrong. It's not the end of the world. Firstly, please understand this: if you tell your team you dislike or disagree with your mentors they will never want to meet them or listen to them, so be careful. That's business suicide and not something I recommend.

Even if you don't like someone, bite your tongue where possible. Someone in your team may love them and you are there to serve your team. Having said that, if there are exceptional circumstances and there is no way for now that you can reconcile your relationship with them, look for other areas where you can gain support.

Build relationships with others who are on a similar path as you and work closely with your parent company. Do not criticise or complain about the person you have any issue with to other people. This will be a huge mistake. Be polite, protect your brand as a person and just agree to disagree for now. In time if you can build bridges, forgive and forget, then that will be a great outcome.

There are two ways you can rise quickly through the higher levels.

You can work like crazy yourself, or you can sponsor a superstar that helps to create momentum in your team. I recommend you shoot for both.

Broke people believe that luck is something that you have no control over and it just happens out of the blue. Rich people understand that luck is something that happens when preparation and opportunity collide and the exciting thing is you can get lucky in Network Marketing but only if you are working at it.

The facts are that most people will be average producers. Much the same as in life. Every now and then you can strike gold and sponsor someone who builds a huge team very quickly, which subsequently impacts your turnover for the better and drives you higher up the income charts.

Now I am not saying that fast growth does not come without its challenges. You will have to work really hard on getting the whole team on track. But trust me, I would take fast growth over slow growth any time.

So is it possible to predict where you can find these future stars? Sadly the short answer to that seems to be no, as I have seen them emerge from all sorts of unpredictable environments. However I do have some advice.

First create a culture and mindset in your team of sponsoring people who are better than you or they currently are. What I mean by better is rather than look for people who are below your social standing, look for people who are above you. For example, a lower league rugby player should approach those around him but also those in the leagues above him. A young person should feel confident in offering their opportunity to an older more established professional. You are not the offer. The opportunity is the offer, so don't feel you need success behind you to talk to people.

Send a message to the marketplace that says you are looking for sharp people as opposed to dummies. You're looking to build a strong team, remember? Keep doing this over and over and in time your team will grow in calibre. Create a winning environment of outstanding achievers and guess what? You will attract achievers.

Then when you strike gold and your team is growing like crazy because you have some young, dynamic people driving the growth, just smile and say: "I guess I am just lucky."

Here are some reasons why people are negative about your new business.

If you are young, here is the number one reason why people will come across as negative about what you want to achieve if they are from your family. As strange as it seems here it is. They love you and are concerned you are getting taken for a ride, so the easiest route is to doubt the very thing you want them to believe in.

You misunderstand their motives, feel angry, insecure and sometimes lose confidence if you don't receive their approval. The best advice I can offer is to hold your nerve, generate some success and prove them wrong.

Dealing with negative opinion and misinformed views about what you do and what you offer.

People doubt or disbelieve in the business because they don't understand what it is. In addition, they may have heard some bad stories about your new venture and this creates fear. They have no positive frame of reference to draw upon, so it's natural they are negative. This has been going on for centuries. Columbus was told he was going to sail off the edge of the world but it didn't stop him from writing his own history.

Once again, the good news is nobody can stop you. Go and create some success. Show them what's possible and then explain the facts later. They are unlikely to listen until you create some success. Stop stamping your feet. You haven't achieved anything yet. Focus on creating results and eventually they will be forced to believe in you.

Dealing with distributors or customers who are a pain.

You create the world you live in and you can change the world you live in at any time you want. Don't moan about dealing with difficult customers or distributors. Either get excited about what you can learn from the situation or get rid of them. It's that simple.

You have to protect yourself from the 'energy vampires'. They will suck the life out of you if you let them.

If you are wasting energy on a situation, it means you are not putting that same energy to work somewhere else in your life.

You are choosing to do this. Don't act like some victim that you want people to feel sorry for because that's not going to help you. Yes you may find someone who is happy to join your personal pity party but is that going to do you any good? I am not sure how long you will choose your state of misery to last but eventually you will get fed up with it and decide it's time to move on. As soon as you do that you will feel like the world has lifted off your shoulders and the rest of your life can begin.

If you don't, it will drive you insane. Wise people learn from everything in life. Good, bad or indifferent. You're not a cow, so my advice is to choose to change your thinking.

No man is a prophet in his own land. The stranger is always the expert.

This is one of those observations that you will only understand when you see it in action. Put another way: people who know you or are familiar with you and your message are unlikely to listen to you. That's just how it is.

I have lost count of the amount of times someone has spoken to my team and told them exactly what I have told them for years, only for them to come back and say: "Did you hear that? How come you never told us that?" I am going to resist screaming! Hey, that's just how it is, so don't get frustrated when it happens to you.

One more thing: the satirical nature of life in the UK and Ireland means people are much more comfortable taking the mickey or gently undermining your message to bring you back down to earth. Don't react. Just understand that's how it is. Keep working on the basics of your model, travel to meet new teams and it will be you that's the stranger with all the knowledge and then finally you will enjoy people acting on exactly what you say.

Elephants can't sew and pigs can't sing. Have you got the right people?

You have to be realistic. Don't waste your time trying to help people who don't want to be helped. Don't sit on them like a chicken trying to hatch an egg. Leave them to become what they have to become. Essentially that title means, was my expectation of an individual's talents and capabilities far too high? Hey, it's good to have high expectations but there comes a point where you can delude yourself. You would not ask a powerlifter to enter a ballet competition. Ultimately, you need the right team around you and you have to be prepared to keep searching. Don't be lazy with this. Surround yourself with great people.

Protecting your mind.

At all costs protect your thoughts. I have positive mental attitude training books and audios with me at all times, reminding me of how I need to act and live. Does the average person do this? No. But here is a clue: I don't want to be average. I want to live an inspired life.

The average person will often pour scorn on you and your attempts to get ahead and improve yourself. If this happens to you, be happy and take it as a compliment. They are letting you know you are different to them. Happy days!

The Society we live in is pretty negative. If you don't believe me, just switch on the news. Doom and gloom is everywhere. If a few people think I am a little nuts then that's great. I want to be happy and I am not going to shoot for anything less.

Get the 'big rocks' of your life in place first.

The rocks in the vase story.

An old teacher stands in front of his classroom. Today the class will get one of the best lessons they have ever had.

At the front of the room he has a large glass cylinder shaped vase. Into the vase he places a number of large rocks, one by one, all the way to the top until it's full.

He then asks the class: "Is the vase full?" "Yes." they all reply.

He then takes a bucket of pebbles. Very carefully the children watch hundreds fall in between the larger rocks but eventually the vase is truly full and no more will go in.

He then asks the class: "Is the vase full?" "Yes." they all reply.

He then takes a bucket of sand, slowly he pours in the sand. Thousands of tiny grains of sand fall between the pebbles and, as before, the vase finally looks full and no more will go in. The students clap, realising how clever their teacher is.

He then asks the class: "Is the vase full?" "Yes." they all reply confidently.

He then takes a bucket of water. Gently he pours in the water until nearly a gallon has soaked in. It's now packed solid.

The children are mesmerised.

"Children", he says. "If you had filled it with water first, it would have all poured out as the sand entered. Once the sand was in it would be almost impossible to get any amount of pebbles in. And would you be able to fit in the big rocks?"

"No Sir, we would not."

"That's correct. I want you to always remember this lesson. As you go forward to create your life you will need to make many decisions and there will be times when you are unsure where your priorities may lay.

For every problem you face I want you to imagine your life is the glass vase. With that in mind I want you to decide what the most important elements of your life are. What are the big rocks that have to go in the vase before anything else regarding each and every project or dilemma you face?

When you follow these guidelines you will always know your priorities and it will help you to keep your life in balance. Pebbles, sand and water represent all the lesser items that make up our life. Never allow them to get in the way of the rocks in your vase."

Today my kids are growing into young adults and I have shared this story with them many times as they have met with temporary confusion in deciding between right and wrong. Try it yourself. It's just a fun, simple illustration to help us all keep things in line with what we want as individuals.

Once you do this you will avoid giving small things any sense of priority. You will see the bigger picture and you will feel balanced and grounded. If you are too busy (full) to fit in the big important things that make you happy, it's a sure fire thing that you have put some sand or pebbles (small unimportant things) in your vase before the rocks.

Finally, let me share just one last crucial detail. Sadly, way too many people have forgotten it's the little things that are really the big things.

Sunset, sunrise, small acts of kindness, good food, good company, great music, beautiful wine, scented candles, a log fire, bluebells and lambs in the fields in spring. I am sure you get the idea. Make your own list. There are riches all around you. Open your mind, your heart and your eyes and life will blow you away.

Life flashes by at light speed so I hope I have grabbed your attention with this book before it's too late. This last chapter will be my attempt to make sense of the madness and chaos that makes up our life. I hope it's entertaining. I hope it scares you a little and I hope it inspires you. It will be deadly honest, that's for sure.

CHAPTER 10

THE HIGHS AND LOWS OF LIFE AS AN ENTREPRENEUR.

The highs and lows of life as an entrepreneur.

Understand this. Your starting point will never be perfect and it will be messy for a long time. That's just how it is. Eventually (and I mean eventually) when you get it all right it can and will be truly spectacular but you have to know that success is a journey not a destination. Get it wrong and there will be times when the pain will drop you to your knees, I have been in both places and know which one I would prefer you to have more of.

Learning to ride the emotional rollercoaster of being your own boss is both exhilarating and challenging. Of course there will be times where you doubt yourself and feel more than a little scared. But equally, there will be amazing moments where all your hard work and self-belief put you in exactly the sweet spot you want to be in life and there is no better feeling of knowing it's you who created it.

Let's start off with the lows.

The reason I want to start here is because that's where the biggest audience tends to be. If you are feeling the pain of not being where you want to be, at some point you have to turn that pain into your motivation for change. For some of you it's just a knowing feeling that there must be another way and for others it's a burning ambition to break free into a new life. Wherever you are on that scale the lessons in this book are important.

Life is tough in so many ways to so many people. You have to take the stones that are thrown at you and use them as your foundations for a better future.

Time and again you are going to get tested and time and again you are going to need to get back up. You will only do that if you have a massive 'this has to happen' attitude.

Here is my kick in the teeth list that hurt like hell but I managed to survive.

I am sharing these personal experiences with you because I know some of you will be suffering from similar issues and I want you to know you can pull through. I am no expert, so seek professional help when your burden is unmanageable. This is about you surviving and moving forward. Here is my list when starting out.

The pain of having no money.

Whether you are young or old, this is not such a bad thing. I was young and broke and used my lack of money to motivate me to go make some. I was driven by the fact that I had nothing in my pockets and if you are in the same situation you should do the same thing.

Sadly, some people link their bank balance to their self-image and believe their lack of money is verification that they are a loser. This is not true. It's verification that you have made some bad decisions that you can change today but only if you really want to.

As you get a little older, throw in some dependents like children and it gets a little more complicated. Some people get frozen by self-doubt, struggling to believe they can ever rise above their problems. They feel they are not only letting themselves down but they are letting others down. Again, this is the voice in your head telling you that you're a loser. Get control of that voice!

You are not a loser. You are whatever you want to be, so choose to change your thinking. Start by changing that voice in your head. Do as I have suggested in this book. Write out some positive affirmations and act on them. I did and it worked for me because I made it work. You can do the same but as ever, only if you really want to!

There is always a way out, please remember that. As long as you keep that thought in your mind above all, you will make it. Remember, as you read these words I want you to know I have experienced all the emotions that I have typed about. I also want to assure you, no matter how dark it gets (and sometimes it will be pitch black) please listen to me. There truly is always a way out. Now go and use what you have learned in this book and make some money.

Fighting over money and the lack of it.

There are few things that destroy the joy in a relationship more than fighting over the lack of money. I have lost count over the fights we have had along the way. I was always trying my best but sometimes trying your best is just not good enough. Trying your best is not the same as having lots of money in the bank. My emotions were in tatters. Why does my wife not believe in me? Doesn't she know I am trying my best? No. She knows there is nothing in the bank account and the kids need clothes and food. That's what she knows!

There is a big difference between trying your best but producing the same results each month, each year and watching life slip away.

Try this instead. Ask yourself what you've learned and what you're committed to change today. Make a decision to get better every day and inside ninety days things can and will look a whole lot better.

Those fights will keep coming until you change your relationship with money. Until you do that you will keep fighting.

Here are a few simple personal finance rules:

1. Spend less than you earn.

2. Learn how to earn more than you need.

3. Apply rule one.

If you don't have it, don't spend it. Live frugally and focus on making money. You won't be broke for long if you apply these rules.

Today life is incomparable to where I started out, so let me give you some examples of where life was to help you realise I relate to anyone's starting position.

Every week I would know the price of petrol at different locations so I could save money each time I filled up.

I knew exactly the difference in price between Tesco's 'no frills' verses the competition. For those who don't know, the 'no frills' stuff is the cheap own-brand one with blue and white stripes on the packaging so everyone at the till knows you're broke.

Be thankful for austerity is all I can say. Now it's cool to shop in Aldi and Lidl. A few of you will get that joke. Those of you still shopping in Waitrose don't need to get the joke so it's ok.

Here is a tough one for me. This one still hurts because I can never go back.

We bought all Georgia's clothes in black bin bags from the yellow page ads. She is now twenty, bright, beautiful and takes my breath away each time I see or speak to her. So don't feel sad as you read this. She was only a baby and knew no different. The clothes had barely been worn. If you are a mum or dad you will know that new clothes cost a fortune and we just did not have the money, so we bought them second-hand.

Hey, no drama. We did what we had to do. I am just letting you know things weren't perfect. I also know there are people all across the planet who struggle to eat each day, so it's no big deal compared to that. Just in case you are feeling a little fragile over not being able to spoil your kids, I do understand.

When the kids got sick (and all kids do), hoping the boss would give us time off without any repercussions also made me feel uneasy. You know the usual unbelievable stuff that happens: "Sorry I am late boss. Georgia was rushed to hospital because she pushed a frozen pea up her nose." True.

Then there is the label shopping. You know. Check the price on the label before trying it on. Reading the menu in the restaurants from right to left, instead of left to right. Come on, keep up. The prices are on the right. I could go on and on but I am sure you got the point. Don't fret over it. Just do something about it.

We did so look out, the grandkids are going to get spoiled big time.

People will lie to you. Learn from it. That's life.

It's just one of the things that will happen that will speed up your learning and hopefully sharpen your mind before the next con artist rolls around.

One of my great mentors Jim Rohn once said: "Hey Jeff. Everyone needs to know a little law. Sign the wrong contract and it could cost you a fortune."

I am not going to use this book as a vendetta against every bad deed done to me but certain stories help to illustrate a point. We had planned to fit an oak balcony along the rear of the house. A stunning piece of 3D design and I was excited about seeing it go up. To save money we were ordering the oak direct from France in containers and then cutting it down. One of the carpenters had previously fitted the oak roof on the house. He rang up and asked if it was ok if we could put the money for this next job into his personal account instead of the business account. I thought nothing of it as they had already done some great work for us and this was the last job. So I transferred the £7500 he had asked for.

After six months of waiting for the carpenter to start the balcony work, following various excuses (including the fact that his mother had died of cancer), Deb said to me she felt uneasy about the situation.

I finally managed to get hold of one of the other carpenters and co-owners. I told him I was sorry for his partner's loss but could not wait any longer for the work to be done. "What do you mean?" he said. "His mother is alive and well!" When I told him I had sent the money six months ago he was astonished and sickened. Needless to say the money was stolen and the next step was court action.

There are people like this in life. Despicable people who lie and cheat their way through life at other people's expense. Do what you can to protect your-self. I am not a naive person but everyone can get caught. Please be careful.

The business lesson to learn is simple. Be careful. Know who you are paying, what you are paying for, stage the payments and keep a very clear paper trail. You will need it if things go wrong. If people promise to provide a service for the money you pay, they are liable in court if the service is not delivered.

Document all that you do in business very clearly so that anyone reviewing your affairs at a later stage in court (if it ever gets that far) can see clearly what was promised and what was agreed. It's difficult to defend your position with no written evidence, so back up all conversations in writing as soon as they have happened.

Lastly, remember to read the terms and conditions of all contracts very care-fully. If there is something you are not happy with you need to raise it and get any corrections required in writing for them to have any substance or mean anything in court. Verbal agreement will not be enough.

Unexpected setbacks.

Expect the unexpected is all I am saying. It's rarely a smooth ride. All sorts of stuff will happen on your journey. Do what you can not to over-expose your-self. It's impossible to plan for every eventuality, I am not denying that. What I am saying is set some money aside as you earn it. Cars and equipment will break down. Cover yourself with insurance on all the important elements of your life and business.

Get the 'big rocks' in place with respect to your finances and paperwork as I have already mentioned and you will be taking a big step in the right direction.

Dealing with life, life threatening illness and the loss of loved ones. What can you learn from tragedy?

Success in business is all about focus. So what happens when your world falls apart? Your world falls apart. That's it, it falls apart and all that was nor-mal yesterday is gone today. Life turns a hundred and eighty degrees in a heartbeat. And what happens to your focus? It's gone. And it's totally gone.

In exercise terms, one of your fitness measurements is how quickly your pulse recovers from intense exercise. Mental toughness can be very similar. We all get knocked down and pushed to our limits emotionally. How quickly you can collect your thoughts will determine your mental fitness and ultimately your ability to recover your focus.

You have to decide to step above or outside any emotional turmoil you are going through. Visualise you can do it. Just as I wrote earlier, see yourself as two separate bodies and step away from the problem as opposed to being consumed by it.

Don't think for a second that I walk through personal tragedy pain free. I don't have a heart made of stone but equally I don't want to be part of the problem. It's tough to stay objective but it's the only way that's worked for me. Take a deep breath, breathe slowly and give it a try. I know it will work for you.

Heart attacks, cancer, suicides, drug abuse, anorexia and alcoholism have all walked in and out of my life in one form or another. Through it all I have tried to learn to be more grateful and love life even more. I am not saying it was easy but I am saying it was worth it. You can do the same.

Leadership can be lonely. The top of the mountain is not crowded.

If you are going to adopt all the leadership points in this book, you are going to be different that's for sure. At some point you are also going to be lonely. You are going to question yourself. You are going to suffer temporary doubt and confusion. It's ok. All leaders who have ever made a stand and achieved anything worthwhile have been in the same place.

Seek out like-minded people and your sanity will quickly return. As you grow you will notice all the things that other people do that you have learned not to do. Over time you will question yourself less and less and eventually you will have a new circle of friends that all stand for the same values.

None of us are robots. Occasionally you will get attacked by temporary loss of belief. Recommit to all you have learned and confidence will return. Be assured you are on the right path. Do not go backwards from here.

Keep your dreams alive at all costs.

Life is frustrating and will pull you in twenty different directions all at once. Learning how to deal with this is a big part of remaining sane. Your ups and downs will live or die by the strength of your dreams. People in touch with their dreams have a sparkle about them. They are alive. You can feel it. People who are just going through the motions have no energy. They can't ignite anything, so nothing happens for them.

Every single person I have come across who has created any form of success in their life did so because they had a burning ambition for their dream to become a reality. There is no hiding the fact that big dreams create big motivation. So what's your dream?

The highs. Use these to motivate yourself and others.

Being inspired by what others have achieved.

Through history, leaders have shown others what's possible. My journey began when someone else showed me that my life could take a very different path to the one I had been programmed to take in my early years. That day changed my life in a profound way. I had no idea what was possible until that moment and I want this book to be the same catalyst for you.

I hesitate in announcing all the highs of being in business for a few reasons, so again let me put in a few disclaimers. This is not me trying to say hey, look how clever I am. It's also not a message that says everyone can achieve this. I am merely trying to highlight the benefits that will come your way if you embrace all the points I have outlined in this book. Success is not achieved by everyone. It's achieved by a small group of people who decide their life will not be a casual affair. It's your choice if you choose to join that exclusive group.

Small victories that build your confidence.

When I started out I was excited, hopeful but also a little fragile. On a weekly basis my emotions would swing between high and low, mostly based on external influences. A few books and seminars later I realised I needed to be internally motivated and get the outside world to dance to my tune. Pretty soon I realised it was a marathon, not a sprint. I learned from each small victory that came my way and you will need to do the same. I learned from my sponsors and other leaders within the industry to analyse what I had done right in order for me to know what to repeat. I had no idea at the time how important this was but now I appreciate it was a critical lesson.

Spoiling loved ones and helping friends out.

It's natural for any entrepreneur to want to work twenty-four seven, so don't forget this one. There are few things that will feel any better than taking care of and spoiling the people you care for. I don't need much to enjoy life but it's great to know there is enough in the bank to take care of those around me. It's not the big things that make the greatest impact on a day by day basis to the people around you, it's the little things. So never forget that.

The freedom to live the way you want.

I just wanted the freedom to do what I wanted to do when I wanted to do it. I hated being owned and controlled by an alarm clock. I didn't want to be a home to work robot who never questioned the path that everyone else was happy to follow each day. For centuries, battles have been fought to obtain and preserve our personal freedom. It's one of our most prized possessions and worth every effort you can invest to gain yours.

Throwing a financial blanket around your family.

Having the peace of mind to know your family is looked after and you no longer need to worry about money is priceless. I have never made money my 'God'. However, not having enough of it in a Western society definitely presents its challenges. Creating a plan that allows you to accumulate enough money to protect yourself and family should be your top priority. Living life to its fullest can be expensive. It costs a significant amount of money to set up any form of household.

I will stop short of offering detailed financial advice but here are a few easy principles to follow.

Focus on keeping your liabilities low and your assets high. Liabilities are anything that consumes your money and assets are anything that creates money for you. Don't live beyond your means. As you make money, don't rush out and drive flashy cars that lose the money you have just fought to earn. Live conservatively until you can buy those items out of petty cash. There is a great little book called The Richest Man in Babylon. Read it and use it as your guide. In time you will be grateful for this advice. Just like many other points in this book it's simple to follow and simple not to follow. That choice is yours.

No more alarm clocks.

This is definitely my favourite and I am sure it will be one of yours. Being able to roll over instead of rolling out on a cold winter's morning is priceless. Being able to chat to the kids on the school run as opposed to being up and away before they wake has made a massive difference in our lives as a family.

They call them alarm clocks because you wake up in a state of alarm. I am also told a high percentage of heart attacks occur on Monday morning. I wonder why. I remember clearly waking up and dreading the journey ahead, being jammed like a sardine into the London underground, stuck in endless traffic, waiting for the delayed trains. None of it was ever fun. All of that goes away when you create financial freedom.

Today nobody is our boss. We decide what we want to do, when we want to do it and it feels fantastic.

Enjoying brief moments of indulgence.

Part of me hates typing this because I don't want to come across as flash in any way but the truth is it's great fun to do now and then. Little things like flying business class and drinking cocktails at the bar on the amazing Airbus A380 on the way to Dubai or Thailand in winter just makes you smile. Knowing you can take a few mates for an awesome meal and pick up the tab makes you feel good. I know it's not the be all and end all of life but it's nice to do and I want you to know that it's not all about work.

Buying flowers for no particular reason, buying little presents or drinking nice wine as opposed to cheap wine. When you're not watching every penny, the little extras make a big difference to the fun you have.

Helping people on their journey.

I absolutely love this bit of my life. I know how much I appreciated every little word of encouragement I had when trying to find my way forward and feel privileged to be able to help anyone with the same ambition. Put yourself in my position and I know you will feel the same way. It was a real scrap to get through all the things I had to get through but it shapes you in so many ways. When you come out the other side of any struggle you feel an amazing sense of self-worth. If I had to do it all again, knowing what I know today I would have worked ten times harder, been ten times happier and concerned myself ten times less with the opinion of others.

Helping people understand this is a big part of getting them through whatever they need to get through. I have lost count of the cards, emails, online messages and conversations I have had from people thanking me for supporting them on their journey. What they often don't realise is the happiness I get from seeing them break the chains. It's fantastic to see someone's confidence grow as a result of your belief in them. For me to have that belief in them I first had to get that belief in me and you are no different. I hope this book teaches you how important that first step really is.

Watching new warriors come through in your team.

This is pearl diving at its best. Warriors are young leaders who are prepared to do whatever it takes. They are raw, unrefined, passionate, emotional and have limitless energy. As I watch the individuals develop in our team, it's great to know where they will get to as long as they continue to learn. It's like being able to live your life all over again. I see so much of how I used to be when I see these leaders emerge. A big part of me wants to protect them and support them but the truth is it's safer to get out of the way. Of course I try and steer them in the right direction but have you ever tried steering a tornado?

Ultimately, despite any amount of intervention and guidance, leaders find a way. It's that simple.

Relationships. Have good people around you.

Few things will impact your life more than the people you associate with. The partner you choose, the friends you socialise with and the business mentors you look up to. All of them will shape your perspective on life.

It's taken me almost all my adult life to realise how fortunate I was in choosing Deb as my wife all those years ago. I can assure you I did not anticipate the impact she would have on my inner development when I first clasped eyes on her. Of course, things aren't perfect. They never are. We have our share of arguments like anyone else but I can honestly say she has made a massive contribution to my happiness and appreciation of life.

Within our business we have an amazing team of kind-hearted, hardworking and fun to be with people. For us it went way past the money we earn a long time ago. We have more income than we could ever have dreamt of and continue to live pretty simple lives. All we want to do now is help our team fulfil whatever their ambitions drive them towards and we enjoy every moment.

Outside of our business we have a diverse group of friends which allows us to enjoy a wide range of company and conversations. The humour is razor sharp. One of the local boys had a terrible accident in work recently which meant he lost his thumb. After the usual concerns and commiserations it wasn't long before he was nick-named "Kit-Kat" because he now has four fingers. As you can tell, it's not a culture for the meek.

The truth is, we would all die for each other and that's why we have learned to laugh in the face of almost every adversity that comes our way.

Understanding the power of being grateful.

We all get caught up in our own world sometimes and lose sight of the bless-ings we have. Take a moment to reflect on the things you are truly grateful for and your heart will start to swell and a gentle smile will appear on your face. I am not sure how this works but it works.

A number of years ago I met a good friend of mine down at the beach. It was a wild but beautiful day. The wind was raging and nature was having its own rock concert as the waves smashed ashore.

John was terminally ill but had a great smile on his face. I said: "Hey John. How are you?" "Fantastic!" he replied back with a big smile. We had a great chat and then I asked him this question: "John. How come you are always happy and smiling despite your condition?"

His reply shook me to my core.

He said: "That's easy Jeff. I changed the word want to have in all my conversations."

Waw! The tears are rolling down my face and I am struggling to type this.

John died not long after and I have never forgotten that conversation. Learn to be grateful, sometimes it's all you will have. Change the word "want" to "have" in all your observations of your life. You already have so much more than others. Learn to appreciate that and you will take a big step towards living your life with a happy heart.

Leave a legacy. Dad left his mark.

Our moment in the sun is fleeting at best. My life is flying by. How fast has the last twelve months of your life passed by? As you get older I promise you it accelerates.

Dad was an avid reader, sometimes four books a week. I have no idea what he would have made of my little attempt but I hope he would have appreciated the sentiment. He was then and remains a guiding force in my life. He was funny, outrageous, kind, generous, warm, gentle, strong and so much more. I keep his spirit close to me every day.

You now have more than enough information. If you follow all you have read about with some passion and enthusiasm anything is possible. Sometimes I wish I could lift the lid off my head and allow you to take a look. It's messy but you will know what I have typed is the truth.

I hope I have done what I set out to achieve. I want you to think carefully about the career choices you make and I want you to see Network Marketing as an exciting and viable option.

The book may be over but your journey has just begun. Go back to the start of the book and read it again. Each time you turn the pages see and feel yourself having grown in confidence and belief. Let the words have greater impact and look deep inside yourself. Slowly you will discover new thoughts and make decisions that change your course.

Don't make the mistake that many will and read it as temporary reassurance or a fleeting glance into a life you could live. I had many false dawns and I have no doubt you will too but if I can get you to stay on the track, I know you will finish the race. Use it as a roadmap to permanent change. Keep it by your side. You can make your life great. It's worth the fight but you will need daily reminders.

Learn to reach out and build new relationships. If you have enjoyed the content buy a copy for a friend and ask them for their opinion. If they like it also you can go forward as a team.

Life is a series of simple choices. Choose carefully. There is a spectacular journey ahead for those who want it to be that way.